LABOUR MARKETS IN THE SUDAN

LABOUR MARKETS IN THE SUDAN

A study carried out within the framework of the
ILO/UNHCR Project on Income-Generating Activities
for Refugees in Eastern and Central Sudan

Ibrahim El-Bagir and Jenny Dey

Ali Abdel Gadir Ali and Tony Barnett

Jayati Ghosh

Albert Wagner

INTERNATIONAL LABOUR ORGANISATION
UNITED NATIONS HIGH COMMISSIONER FOR REFUGEES

INTERNATIONAL LABOUR OFFICE   GENEVA

ISBN 92-2-103749-5

First published 1984

Printed in Switzerland

The present volume prepared for publication by Jayati Ghosh provides a summary of the studies of the three major labour markets in Sudan: in urban areas, in rainfed agriculture, and in irrigated areas (the Gezira). These studies were carried out in the framework of the UNHCR/ILO project on Income Generating Activities for Refugees in Sudan. The approach followed by this project made it necessary to study the Sudanese labour markets as a background to providing durable solutions to the problem of refugees. This approach goes beyond the traditional relief approach and certainly does not give much credence to "the embroidery approach" which recommends unviable activities for refugees. Instead the starting point of this approach was to find income generating activities based on self-employment and integration in the local labour markets.

The genesis of the project however did not preclude the possibility of extending the scope of the study to provide a full-fledged survey of the Sudanese labour markets given the lacuna of studies in this area and with a view to understanding the recent developments of the major labour markets in Sudan. Thus, three surveys were carried out covering the three major labour markets, complemented by two limited-scope surveys: one on labour camps and another on emigration.

The picture that emerged from these surveys is one of labour markets in transition. This results from a combination of a number of factors: on the one hand, the massive emigration of Sudanese to Saudi Arabia and the Gulf (estimates vary but they are never below 15 per cent of the labour force) has created a shortage of skilled and, to a lesser extent, unskilled labour; stagnation of the traditional sectors of the economy both in agriculture and industry contrasted with an expansion of the services sector catering for the demand created mainly by remittances; and the lack of a consistent set of policies for intervention in the labour markets. Despite a recent deceleration in economic activity in the oil-rich economies projections show that emigration from Sudan will continue well into the 1990s. The structure of demand for Sudanese labour may change with the change in the pattern of investment in the oil economies, but the demand for Sudanese labour will continue. Given this situation where emigration represents both a skill and a brain-drain on the one hand and the country's major foreign exchange source on the other hand, the study of the impact of emigration on the labour markets becomes extremely essential. Moreover, the stagnation of the Sudanese economy since the mid-1970s had far-reaching implications for the allocation and remuneration of labour in both the urban and rural areas. As the three studies presented in this volume show, the picture of the labour markets is a complex one. First, the non-market and institutional factors continue to be important in determining labour use despite the constant commercialisation of the Sudanese economy. Second, the shift in the structure of effective demand as a result of changing tastes and the change in income distribution has influenced the demand for various categories of labour especially in the urban areas. Finally, there are strong linkages between the rural and the urban labour markets. Notwithstanding this complex situation, there has been a lack of consistent policies to deal with the various imbalances in the labour markets created by economic stagnation and emigration. It is hoped that the present studies, which represent a comprehensive attempt to understand the working of the Sudanese labour market, point to the gaps in the knowledge for which further work is required, and provide a long-awaited background for policy interventions.

Samir Radwan
Project Manager
International Labour Office

Acknowledgments

This study is very much the product of collective work - a large number of people have contributed to it at various stages. The project was organised and directed by Samir Radwan, who also provided guidance at each stage of the research and commented on the written drafts. Our warmest thanks are due to H.E. Ambassador Abdel Magid Beshir Elahmadi, the Commissioner of Refugees, and H.E. Mohammed El-Murtada Mustafa, the Commissioner of Labour of the Government of Sudan. None of the research embodied in this book would have been possible without their constant support, assistance and encouragement, which went far beyond even the very generous traditions of Sudanese hospitality.

Much logistic assistance and help in organising and conducting the field surveys was provided by Mohammed Tahir Mageit (Labour Office, Khartoum), El-Tireifi Younis and Ismael Ibrahim (Office of the Commissioner of Refugees in Shwak and Gedaref), Abdel Gadir (Office of the Commissioner of Refugees in Port Sudan), Taha El Jack Taha, Saddig al Beshir Ahmed (Sheikh of Nueila village, Gezira), Abdel Wahab Ali Modawi (Department of Statistics, Khartoum), Abdel Gadir Al Mardi (Personnel Director, Kenana Sugar Company) Ahmed Osman (ESRC Khartoum) and Abdel Mejid Hussein. In Khartoum, Abdul Moneim, Rogaia Mustafa Khojali, Khalid Hassan Mutwali, Abdelaziz Sayed El-Tayeb and the rest of the staff at the Labour Office, as well as Mustafa Fakih and Mervat Abdelaziz of the Office of the Commissioner of Refugees, all unstintingly gave a great deal of practical help.

In Geneva our work would not have been possible without the constant support and encouragement of, as well as the excellent facilities provided by Jack Martin (Chief, Employment and Development Department, ILO) and Dharam Ghai (Chief, Rural Employment Policies Branch, ILO). Albert Wagner and Patrick Cornu dealt with the work of data processing and computation. Special thanks are due to Lesley Brooks, Geraldine Ople and Sandra Deacon who have borne the brunt of typing various versions of this study, with patience, efficiency and good humour. They were assisted at various stages by Heather Mitches, Irene Pearson, Lynda Pond, Jane Barrett and Kareen Hayes. Evelyn Schaad provided invaluable bibliographic assistance, which greatly facilitated the writing of the chapters. Anne Marie Causanillas cheerfully bore the substantial burden of administrative work in Geneva and Khartoum.

The many flaws that remain in this study are notwithstanding the critical comments we have, received from a number of perceptive observers. At a workshop held in Khartoum in April 1983, Ali Mohammed El-Hassan and Ali Abdel Gadir Ali gave insightful and useful comments on earlier versions of the chapters. Additional comments which we have tried to incorporate have been made by Adel Beshai, Mohammed Mirghani and Simon Commander.

Finally, it is hoped that the present volume fulfills the twin objectives of providing Sudanese planners and policy makers with a long-awaited knowledge base for labour market intervention policies, and stimulating further research for a fuller understanding of the functioning of the labour markets in Sudan.

Table of Contents

PART I:

THE BACKGROUND

CHAPTER 1

Macro-Economic Processes and Labour Markets
in Sudan: An Overview

A study of labour markets can imply a notion of the prior commercialisation of labour within an economy, such that the manner of exchange of labour as a commodity has become the dominant expression and determinant of the labour process. However, such an overarching assumption would be unwarranted in the case of Sudan (as also for many other largely rural developing countries). Here, many of the productive activities which constitute the labour process are organised not on market principles but on a more informal, flexible set of arrangements which allow for self-employment as well as forms of non-market labour trading within and between households. This is true not only of the traditional agricultural sector in the rural areas, but of many forms of urban employment.

In this volume, attempts have been made to incorporate the analysis of non-market labour processes, so as to provide a more complete picture of the nature of productive employment in the various economic sectors. Nevertheless, the focus remains on labour markets, for three principal reasons. Firstly, Sudan has witnessed historically a process of commercialisation of labour, beginning in the early part of this century with labour recruited for irrigated agricultural schemes, and including the fairly recent emergence of the use of hired labour in large-scale mechanised rain-fed agriculture, along with the growth of urban wage employment. These labour markets display some of the important features of labour processes in each sector. Secondly, the behaviour of the various labour markets indicates not only the geographical movement of labourers but also, and more importantly, the points of inter-sectoral linkage between different economic activities. Thirdly, the labour markets reflect the macro-economic tendencies and processes which govern the behaviour of the economy as a whole, and in their turn react upon these processes.

The chapters which follow deal in detail with the nature and functioning of labour markets in the three main economic sectors: rainfed agriculture, irrigated agriculture and urban industrial and other activities. Each of these chapters is based on a separate survey carried out in specific areas of central and eastern Sudan, in the latter part of 1982. These studies isolate the particular features and mechanisms which govern the labour market and labour processes in the different sectors. Nevertheless, together they tell a common story, the essentials of which are related below.

Any discussion of labour markets in Sudan must be placed in the context of movements in the whole economy. Some years ago it was common to characterise Sudan as the "potential breadbasket of the Arab world", on the verge of an economic breakthrough which would substantially increase per capita GNP as well as the level of development. Sudan's relatively small population, the extremely favourable man-land ratio,[1] one of the world's largest areas of hiterto untapped potentially arable land and other natural wealth, including some recently discovered oil reserves, all contributed to this impression. Notwithstanding these advantages, Sudan remains one of the world's least developed countries, in terms of such criteria as GDP per capita and its rate of growth, the level of industrialisation, the level of literacy, etc. Furthermore, over the last decade the Sudanese economy has been plagued by many problems common to less developed countries, often in a more extreme form. These have accentuated the problems of slow and uneven development within the country, as well as brought its external economic condition to a situation rapidly assuming crisis proportions.

In the last few years output in agriculture has remained almost constant or else has increased by only a small percentage. Cotton, wheat and sesame production have fallen significantly over the decade.[2] This has been due largely to the stagnation of traditional rainfed agriculture and falling productivity of land in the irrigated schemes, primarily the Gezira. The only major increase has been in sugarcane production, largely as a result of the setting up of the Kenana plantation near Kosti. There has been some new investment in irrigated schemes (Rahad and Suki) but by far the greatest proportion of agricultural investment has been in the form of the expansion of acreage under large-scale mechanised rainfed agriculture. Most of this has been in the central and eastern areas of Sudan, with the exception of the Habila scheme in Kordofan in the western region. This has involved some increase in agricultural employment, but not to an extent sufficient to counteract the growing requirements of income and employment for sheer economic survival, from the ranks of the traditional peasantry. The expansion of mechanised rain-fed agriculture has also meant encroachment onto the traditional grazing and herding areas of nomadic pastoralist groups, and led to their consequent displacement. Thus the economic condition of rural groups - whether agricultural or pastoral - on the whole has been declining.

This has involved a growing rural push into the cities. The rates of rural-urban migration have been very high in the past[3] and the worsening situation in some rural areas indicates that this will continue in the near future. However, the growth in the urban population as a result of rural-urban migration has not been matched by a concomitant increase in urban industrial employment. In fact, the industrial sector, and manufacturing in particular, have fared rather badly in the recent period. Industrial investment has been limited, and overall industrial production has reamined virtually stagnant over the last decade.[4] At present there is low capacity utilisation in most manufacturing establishments.[5] In some industries this can be traced to demand problems (e.g. textiles and processed foods) but in addition, industrial operation in Sudan faces continuing problems of lack of fuel, electricity shortages and cuts, lack of availability of imported raw materials and spare parts. These adversely affect the investment inclinations of the domestic bourgeoisie, for whom the booming areas are construction (house-building), services and commercial activities both domestic and international. Private foreign capital in Sudan (mainly that of Arab banks and private Arab investors) has been interested primarily in developing the mechanised agricultural sector; this has contributed to both regional and sectoral imbalances.

The poor performance of the agricultural sector and the numerous problems facing the industrial sector have meant that since 1975/76 there have been negative growth rates for all sectors, and consequently a declining GDP in real terms. Added to this dismal domestic economic performance, there has been a growing foreign exchange crisis. The current account deficit has grown steadily since 1971/72, until by 1981/82 the deficit had reached a level of nearly 311 million Sudanese pounds[6] (approximately 240 million dollars). In December 1982 Sudan's total foreign debt was more than $6 billion, and the current account deficits are now augmented by the massive repayments that are necessary (especially since many of the debts were contracted on relatively hard terms). Thus the projected debt-service ratio for 1984/85 (ratio of total interest and debt payments to exports) is as high as 70 per cent.[7] The serious foreign exchange problems have also implied growing reliance on the finances (and consequent acceptance of the dictates) of the International Monetary Fund. In 1982 this led to the adoption of a standard IMF-prescribed policy package: devaluation of the Sudanese pound (by 31 per cent in December 1982), removal of subsidies on essential consumer goods and agricultural inputs and curtailment of public expenditure, as part of the financial austerity measures.

Within this picture of overall economic stagnation, there are two indices that show great buoyancy. The first is that of prices. In the last few years Sudan has experienced high rates of inflation: thus, the urban cost-of-living index for lower-salaried Sudanese

increased by nearly 700 per cent over the decade of the 1970s.[8]
Some of this corresponds to the domestic stagnation now increasingly
characteristic of many less-developed non-oil-exporting countries.
However, there can be no doubt that changes in the price level have
been influenced also by the inflow of remittances (through both
official and unofficial channels) from Sudanese nationals working
abroad. This is the other index which has exhibited substantial
dynamism. It is now estimated that there are more than 1 million
Sudanese working abroad, mostly in Saudi Arabia, but also in Libya,
Kuwait and the Gulf countries.

In effect, what makes the situation in Sudan at once so complex
and so interesting is that, notwithstanding a macro-economic context
of stagnation in production, there has been an increase in effective
demand, due mainly to the impact of remittances from Sudanese
nationals working abroad. The effects of the substantial labour
emigration in recent years from Sudan to the Arab oil-exporting
countries, and their implications for the behaviour of the labour
markets, are discussed in Chapter 4.[9] Remittances have had numerous
direct and indirect effects on the economy and on labour markets, but
one of their primary effects has been to shift the pattern of
effective demand. In the urban economy, but also in certain rural
areas particularly in the central and eastern regions, certain types
of demand have flourished: for example for house-building, consumer
durables and services, including non-essential services. This,
combined with the declining demand for some "traditional" products
(including textiles) and services, has exacerbated the problem of
imbalanced investment and growth within the economy. Thus, the
general picture of economic stagnation does not capture the dynamism
of particular sectors.

The question arises here of why this positive injection,
remittance income, has not acted as an agent of growth and lifted the
economy out of its present trough. The answer is complex, but some
possible explanations are proposed below. Firstly, the level of

remittances has not been as high as would be expected given the numbers of Sudanese working abroad. In 1979/80, remittances recorded offically amounted to US$70 million, 33 per cent of total private transfers. During the late 1970s, remittances, including the value of goods imported under the nil-value scheme, averaged at 10-20 per cent of imports. Even within these, many of the nil value imports were consumer durables such as cars and domestic electrical appliances and equipment, which in turn involved further foreign exchange expenditure for fuel, spare parts, etc.[10]

Secondly, in the last few years of the 1970s there was actually a decline in the level of remittances[11] and there is reason to believe that since then remittances have stagnated or further declined. Some of this may be due to a shift in the pattern of migration, as more migrants take their families with them or seek to settle for longer periods abroad.[12] But a more important reason could be the increasing reliance of emigrants on unofficial channels to remit money and consumer goods. The government's monetary and credit policies, including the acceptance of parallel exchange markets, and the desire to avoid taxation on the part of those receiving money, have operated as disincentives on the legal transfer of foreign exchange earned abroad. This not only limits the government's control over the inflow of foreign exchange, but also affects the pattern of expenditure of such remittances domestically. This is because only relatively small amounts at a time can be sent through unofficial channels, so that such money is unlikely to be used for large-scale productive investment. It is more easily utilised for purposes of house construction, consumption and petty trading.

The basic macro-economic features described above are all related to a general tendency which governs both the behaviour of the different sectors and the functioning of labour markets: the increasing induction of Sudan into the international economic system. The internationalisation of the Sudanese economy has three main aspects. Firstly, the massive external debt, high rate of debt service and increasing balance of payments problems have their own momentum. They require an ever-increasing reliance of foreign aid and other capital account transfers to meet the payments gap. This in turn increases the country's vulnerability, as it implies further borrowing from providers of hard loans or acceptance of external "guidance" of domestic economic policies to obtain grants or loans. The recent application of the standard IMF policy package is one example of such acquiescence to external pressure. The second aspect of involvement in the international economy relates to the fact that a major proportion of investment in the Sudanese economy recently has been foreign investment, whether public or private. The most important investors have been Kuwaitis and Saudi Arabians, and such investment as been overwhelmingly concentrated in the mechanised agricultural sector, especially in increasing the production of foodgrains with a view to exporting output to Arab markets. The third feature is the absorption of Sudan into the Arab labour market, through the relatively large-scale emigration of labour to work in the oil-exporting countries of the Middle East.

These general tendencies help to determine not only the functioning of the various labour markets but also the relations between them. Sudan's population of around 20 million is predominantly (approximately 3/4) rural. In 1980 the active labour force within the country was estimated to number nearly 6 million people. This labour force is divided into the three main sectors characterised earlier; within each sector there are further divisions relating primarily to the type of employer. Diagram 1 below shows the main divisions as well as the direction of labour movement. This movement has always been substantial - both geographically and across sectors. Approximately four-fifths of total internal migration is estimated to be within the rural sector,[13] primarily in the form of seasonal migration for work in irrigated and rainfed mechanised schemes by traditional farmers and pastoralists. Traditional peasants form the majority of rural workers. They are involved in the cultivation of dura and sesame, and also in the production of gum arabic in the western regions. They are also increasingly important suppliers of wage labour in the irrigated schemes and in the large

DIAGRAM 1: Movements between the main labour markets

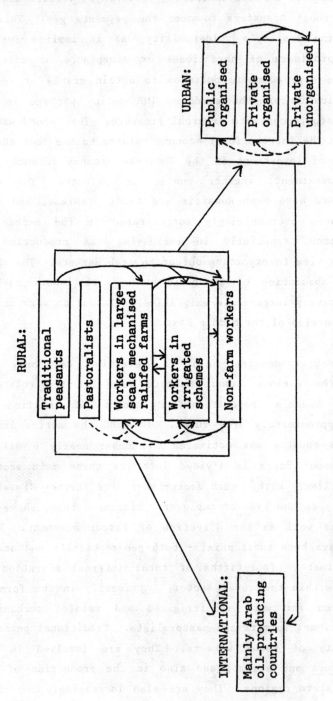

URBAN:
- Public organised
- Private organised
- Private unorganised

RURAL:
- Traditional peasants
- Pastoralists
- Workers in large-scale mechanised rainfed farms
- Workers in irrigated schemes
- Non-farm workers

INTERNATIONAL:
- Mainly Arab oil-producing countries

Notes: 1. The arrows indicate the movement of labour.
2. The dotted lines show quantitatively weaker relationships.

rainfed mechanised agricultural schemes. To some extent, as Chapter 2 indicates, this traditional sector has a dialectical relationship with the new mechanised agricultural schemes. On the one hand, since they produce the same goods, they are in competition in the output market. This contradiction is reinforced by the encroachment by mechanised schemes onto lands traditionally held by small peasant agriculture. On the other hand, the large schemes rely fairly heavily on seasonal agricultural labour (especially for harvesting dura and sesame) for which the primary source is traditional peasant households. This symbiotic relationship between modern and traditional agricultural sectors at once allows for the perpetuation of traditional agriculture (by providing supplementary income for peasant households) and its stagnation at a low level of development (through lack of investment and competition from more modern sectors).

The situation of nomadic pastoralists is somewhat different. Previous estimates put this group at nearly one-fourth of the rural labour force. However, their numbers have been shrinking due to natural and man-made problems, and a recent estimate claims that only about 12 per cent of the rural population is nomadic.[14] The relations between nomadic and settled populations can be characterised as in Diagram 2, when the traditional grazing areas are unaffected by either climatic adversity or competition from other forms of production. This diagram takes account of internal differentiation of the various populations.[15]

DIAGRAM 2: Relations Between Nomadic and Settled Populations in Sudan

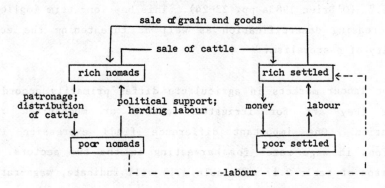

The demand for labour, whether in return for cash, patronage or cattle <u>within</u> the nomadic sector is very limited. When climatic conditions are favourable (which has not been the case in recent years in Sudan) it could be expected that the animal population, and thus the demand for labour within the nomadic system, would increase. By contrast, during periods of climatic adversity, not only will both the human and animal populations face stress, but also the poorer sections of the nomadic community will find it particularly difficult to exchange their labour within the community, or to live off the few cattle which they possess. Such people may be forced to seek wage employment in order to supplement their already meagre level of life, possibly having sold their relatively few cattle first; or they may move out of the nomadic system entirely, becoming settled cultivators. Some seek work locally, in the traditional rainfed agricultural areas, some in the relatively newly developed mechanised rainfed agricultural schemes, some very few may migrate to urban centres. Historically a significant proportion have provided seasonal (cotton-picking) labour in the irrigated schemes.[16] The development of mechanised rainfed cultivation on an extensive scale over the last 30 years has impinged upon the land of both nomadic groups and settled agriculturalists. For pastoralists, this rendered an already precarious existence even more difficult, adding man-made adversity to climatic vicissitudes, and contributing a further push element to seasonal migration for work. A recent discussion of the capitalisation of agriculture has pointed out that "in addition to conflicts over shrinking prime pasture areas, many nomads have been forced into ecologically marginal grasslands and/or the overgrazing of pasture." (O'Brien 1983a pp. 23-24). This has long term implications for increasing desertification as well as threatening the economic viability of pastoralism.

The labour markets in agriculture differ primarily according to whether they are for irrigated schemes or mechanised rainfed cultivation. One important difference finds expression in the variations in wage rates for harvesting in the two sectors. As a comparison of table 2.17 and table 3.13 will indicate, wage-rates for cotton picking are considerably lower than those for harvesting _dura_ and sesame. This finding is consistent with other estimates which calculate a wage differential of around 50 per cent between the two types of agricultural labour. To some extent this is related to the nature of the work: cotton-picking is less arduous than _dura_ and sesame harvesting, and can be performed by women and children as well as adult men. However, a more important factor is the nature of the workforce in the two sectors. As O'Brien (1983b p. 25) has argued, "cotton picking wages have been relatively low because so many of the cotton pickers worked in family groups in which several family members earned incomes to meet the consumption needs of the family. Conversely, wage rates in the rainfed schemes have been relatively higher because the work force there has been composed principally of individuals who leave their families at home and go out in search of an income to help meet the family's consumption needs." The irrigated schemes have traditionally attracted labour from among nomadic pastoralists as well as traditional cultivators from the western region, and both of these categories have generally included women participating prominently in agricultural/pastoral work. This has meant that the irrigated schemes have been able to draw upon a labour supply composed of heterogenous yet connected members, usually family groups comprising men, women and children. By contrast, the new rainfed schemes (and even some of the new cotton-growing schemes) have had to attract labour, often from among the traditional peasantry in the north and east where women are more strictly secluded, and migratory or seasonal agricultural wage-labour is seen as an adult male activity. They have thus had to offer relatively higher wages than the older irrigated schmes, simply to ensure a secure supply of labour. [This does not mean that wages in such new schemes are very high: on the contrary, as Chapter 2 will show, such wages usually provide only the bare subsistence minimum and do not appear to have increased at all in real terms in recent years.]

It has been argued[17] that the differences between labour markets in these two systems of production are now breaking down, paving the way for the formation of a "national" labour market in

Sudan. The labour markets in the different sectors do possess their
individual characteristics and methods of remuneration, bargaining and
control, as the following chapters indicate. However, the process of
internationalisation   of   the   economy,   with   its   associated
capitalisation of agriculture, has meant that the non-market criteria
determining employment have weakened in scope and importance. This is
evident also in the urban economy, where the public sector pay policy
can no longer be said to be the dominant influence in determining
urban wage differentials and trends.   The patterns of labour
emigration and the resulting shortages of skilled and professional
workers, as well as the high turnover rates of unskilled labour, all
reflect the growing domination of the market in urban labour processes.

A word here about labour shortages. The complaint of unskilled
labour shortages in agriculture (especially in the irrigated schemes
but also in the larger rainfed schemes) has been a common one in the
recent past; in fact this is frequently one of the causes to which is
attributed the poor performance of agricultural output. The high
rates of turnover and absenteeism in many urban industries could also
suggest a shortage of unskilled labour in the urban economy. However,
the studies in this volume suggest that this is a misleading argument,
at best a partial reflection of the reality. There _are_ unskilled
labour shortages, but these are related essentially to the prevailing
wage rates, rather than the physical absence of labourers. The point
is that real wages for unskilled labour in many activities are not
"market-clearing" in the sense that they are simply too low to ensure
a continuous and stable supply of workers. Thus, even while the
stagnation and decline of traditional agriculture and pastoralism
create a pool of proletarians available for work, many of the sectors
employing workers have not exhibited any dynamism in real wage rates.
This translates into "shortages" because of the growing availability
of alternative sources of income and employment, primarily through
emigration and in the urban "informal" and service sectors.

The rigidity of real wage rates (remarkable in both irrigated[18] and mechanised rainfed agriculture, as well as in urban organised industries) for unskilled and semi-skilled labour, reflects a deeper structural imbalance within the economy. Thus, wage rates are low, not simply because of the perversity of some employers, but because of the increasing pressures on the viability of particular economic activities. Tenant cultivators producing cotton, as well as urban employers in the textiles, leather and other "traditional" industries, face problems of declining profitability. The shifts in domestic income distribution have adversely affected these traditional urban industries, while the declining export market for cotton and the consequent slump in its price have formed a major part of the difficulties in domestic raw cotton production, thus affecting the profitability of tenant cultivation in the irrigated schmes. To some extent, therefore, the low wage rates in irrigated agriculture as well as in some traditional urban industries, may reflect the sheer inability to bear higher labour costs, over and above the natural tendency of capital to increase the rate of exploitation.

These problems are exacerbated by the imbalanced nature of state plan allocations and private (largely foreign) investment, both sectorally and regionally. Capital has been slow to move out of traditional areas but it still remains sectorally confined. Also, some regions in the West and the South have not been getting sufficient investment, whether agricultural or industrial.

This brings out the point which is, in effect, the main argument of this chapter: the behaviour of labour markets - wage rates, conditions of work, level of employment, shortages and over-supply - is critically affected by movements in the whole economy, particularly changes in income distribution and structural shifts in internal and external demand. This does not ignore the importance of more micro-economic and intra-household factors in determining labour use and factor allocation, as well as availability for wage employment. But this set of studies on labour markets in Sudan may have interest not only for the information it provides on labour movements and labour use within the Sudanese economy. It also provides an example of how macro-economic processes, and in particular those resulting from the growing internationalisation of the economy, affect the terms and conditions of domestic rural and urban employment.

Footnotes

[1] Around 7 persons per square km. in 1980, using 1973 Census projections.

[2] See IBRD (1982) Chapter 2 for a more detailed description of the behaviour of agricultural production indices.

[3] 4.27 per cent increase per annum to Greater Khartoum alone, in the period 1955/56 to 1973/74. See Oberai (1975).

[4] In the decade of the 1970s, the production oc cement, textiles, flour and petroleum products actually declined, while the production of vegetable oils and sugar showed marginal increases. IBRD (1982).

[5] A survey carried out in Khartoum in 1981 estimated that over two-thirds of the factories surveyed operated at below 50 per cent of capacity. IBRD (1982). Similarly low rates were evident in factories visited in Khartoum and Port Sudan in late 1982 - see Chapter 4.

[6] "Briefings" pp. 65-69, Review of African Political Economy No. 26, July 1982.

[7] IBRD (1982).

[8] Statistics from the Department of Labour, Khartoum. "Lower-salaried" refers to those earning below £S500 per year.

[9] See also Appendix 1 to Chapter 3, on labour emigration from a village in the Gezira scheme.

[10] Thus, for example, between 1973 and 1979 the total vehicle fleet in Sudan nearly doubled from 68,000 to 127,000. Of this increase, nearly 60 per cent were passenger cars, mostly registered in the Khartoum area, and usually imported under the nil value scheme. IBRD (1982, p. 19).

[11] The monetary value of remittances was US$79 million in 1977/78 and US$70 million in 1979/80. This obviously implied an even greater decline in real terms.

[12] See Chapter 4 for a discussion of this possibility.

[13] See Chapter 2.

[14] Estimate for 1982, Statistical Abstract of Sudan 1981, p. 11.

[15] Diagram 2 and the following brief discussion are the contributions of Tony Barnett.

[16] O'Brien (1983b).

[17] Ibid., pp. 27-33.

[18] Ali Abdel Gadir Ali (1983) has argued that excess demand for labour in the Gezira scheme is completely a result of the unjustifiably low real wage rates.

PART II:

THE RURAL SECTOR

Contributors:

Ali Abdel Gadir Ali
Anthony Barnett

Ibrahim El-Bagir
Jennie Dey

Albert Wagner

CHAPTER 2

Rural Labour Markets in the Rainfed
Farming Areas of Eastern Sudan

I. Introduction

In labour market studies, analysis is generally focused on evaluating the performance of the market (participation rates, unemployment and underemployment, supply and demand, and wage rates) in terms of such criteria as growth and equity. However, this approach has three serious limitations for an adequate analysis of labour use in rural areas.

The first stems from the fundamental problem of differentiating between economic and non-economic activities. To which category should we allocate tasks which are generally carried out by unpaid family labour and do not have a market wage rate, such as threshing and pounding grain, fetching water for domestic purposes or for livestock, collecting fuel, repairing huts and fencing compounds? While such a distinction was unnecessary in studies of subsistence economies, it has become the cornerstone of the market theorists' analyses of the incorporation of rural societies into the market economy. However, the distinction is to a large extent artificial since it reflects the theorists' need for simplification and a clear-cut division between activities according to whether or not they can be assigned a monetary value, regardless of the possibility that they may also have important non-monetary values. This is also often apparent in discussions of the sexual division of labour whereby many types of work which are exclusively female are considered non-economic per se unless they bring a marketable output. These problems generally result in a gross underestimation of non-market, subsistence activities and the real contribution of the people performing them to the household economy. For this reason we prefer not to attempt such a distinction between economic and non-economc activities and the associated participation rates in these activities, but rather to examine the different ways in which men, women and children contribute to household income and welfare.

A second problem inherent in rural labour market studies is that of defining underemployment given the sharp fluctuations in seasonal demand for labour characteristic of different types of occupation in rural areas. To some extent this is also a problem created by the artificial distinction between economic and non-economic activities: the rural way of life generally allows little leisure. However, in some rural communities there may be special cases of young men who have insufficient qualifications to find the well-paid, generally urban-based, jobs to which they aspire, but who are no longer prepared to contribute much labour to the family farm or take wage employment in agriculture.

The important question is not, in our opinion, to measure the extent of employment or underemployment as such but rather to assess the ability of different categories of rural people to produce enough to meet their basic needs, the constraints on increasing income among the poorest groups, and the ways in which they, in particular, can be helped to escape from the abject poverty in which most of them live. The crucial issue then becomes one of increasing returns to labour which in turn depends on increasing access to land, capital, new technologies, education, supporting services, new or improved inputs and non-farm employment.

The third limitation in conventional labour market analyses stems from the conceptual problem of measuring remuneration for labour in rural areas. The problem arises from the wide and complex variety of the "kind" components of the total income, which may include such diverse items as food (cultivated or gathered), non-food field and tree crops, fish, livestock and its produce, fuel, water, building and furnishing materials, board and keep, land, clothes, jewellery, dowries and bridewealth, social security and training. The failure to take into account fully the importance and complexity of the kind component has often led to three types of problems in the analysis of rural incomes:

(a) Practical difficulties in measuring the kind component often result in it being ignored or seriously underestimated.

(b) In order to compare the kind and cash components or to estimate total income, the former are generally converted into monetary values based on market prices. This not only presents a problem in the choice between sale and purchase price or in computing prices for goods rarely exchanged for cash (all of which would fluctuate seasonally) but also these monetary values do not always reflect the true value of the kind component as perceived by the recipient. In many cases, either because of scarcity or lack of cash, the items received in kind would otherwise have been foregone. Conversely, the cash component may have more importance to the recipient than its cash value might indicate depending on the proportion it represents of his or her total cash income, cash needs, and other opportunities to earn cash.

(c) The sexual division of labour and the nature of decision-making and control of income within the household determine who gets what. In the case of a family farm the (male) household head would invariably control the crops and any cash income derived from crop sales. While the dependent men, women and children who had contributed farm labour would benefit in varying degrees from the kind element of the total income they would generally have no rights to any of the cash income and would receive only whatever the household head wished to give them.

These limitations inherent in many labour market studies often emerge from a macro-type approach to the subject. To avoid these we have started with a micro-level perspective from which we attempt to generalise. The need for such an approach stems from the fact that rural economies are highly differentiated. Our analysis is therefore based on an examination of the characteristics of this differentiation and its implications for understanding the operation of the rural labour market. Four main features of this differentiation are focused on in this analysis.

(a) The distribution of resources (land, labour, capital, skills) according to socio-economic category and the ways in which these are utilised to generate income and/or create employment.

(b) The division of labour within the household by gender and age which is also affected by and in turn affects access to resources and income. This may vary according to the different socio-economic categories mentioned above.

(c) The mix of different farm and non-farm occupations within the household or held by one individual. This may vary according to socio-economic category and the division of labour within the household.

(d) The different forms of market and non-market labour use and remuneration (paid and unpaid family labour, exchange labour, wage labour, communal labour, etc.).

This chapter has two purposes. The first, more general one, is to examine the characteristics, maladjustments and trends in the rural labour market in the rainfed farming area of Eastern Sudan, looking in particular at the ways in which different socio-economic groups are affected by these processes. The second purpose is to improve our understanding of the opportunities for agricultural wage labour open to migrants and refugees living in the area and the conditions of such work, and to consider the implications for labour legislation.

The chapter is based on three complementary studies: a household survey of labour use and income in three villages, a second survey of employed and unemployed agricultural labourers, and thirdly interviews with government and bank officials and some commercial farmers. Since the surveys were carried out in the rainy season when access to villages off asphalt roads is very difficult, villages near the Khartoum-Port Sudan road were selected. These were representative of different tribal groups and farming conditions: some details of the villages are given in the next section.

In Mereibia 82 households were surveyed, representing 26 per cent of the total number of households. The sample was drawn proportionately from different occupational groups and according to the distribution of male and female-headed households. Ninety households were surveyed in Rawashda (15 per cent of the total). The village elders divided the village into rich, medium and poor households and the sample was selected proportionately from these. In Gadambaliya the sample consisted of 124 households (15 per cent of the total) which were chosen proportionately from the two parts of the village.

A young man and a young woman from the area were hired to spend several days in different households in Mereibia and Rawashda, carrying out detailed time budget studies of men's and women's work. These sources of information were supplemented by interviews with village leaders and some male and female farmers.

The survey of employed and unemployed agricultural labourers covered the economic circumstances which led them to look for this type of work, their recent work histories, the wage bargain and conditions of work. In all, 265 seasonal labourers were interviewed in the Gedaref area. The majority (66 per cent), who were unemployed at the time of the survey, were interviewed in or near mechanised farmers' offices in Gedaref when they came for payment or to look for work. The rest of the labourers were interviewed in the evenings in the employers' camps on the farms. Although there may be a slight bias against non-Arabic speakers (10 were interviewed through interpreters) there is no reason to believe that the sample is unrepresentative.

Finally, a series of detailed interviews were held with officials from the Ministry of Agriculture, the Labour Office, and Mechanised Farming Corporation, the Agricultural Bank of Sudan, the Bank of Khartoum, the South Gedaref Farmers' Union and some commercial farmers.

The following section examines the socio-economic differentiation within the survey villages which leads to two quite distinct farming systems: smallholder and large mechanised production units. In Section 3 the labour strategies of different socio-economic groups and the implications of the interaction of the two farming systems on the rural labour market are analysed. The position of the migrant and refugee seasonal agricultural labourers in the labour market and their conditions of work are discussed in Section 4. The recommendations are set out in the final section.

II. Socio-economic differentiation

Background

The three survey villages, representing a range of tribal groupings with different historical backgrounds, were selected so as to highlight the various socio-economic factors which account for significant differences between the two major farming systems in the rainfed areas of Eastern Sudan: large-scale mechanised commercial farming and smallholder subsistence and cash crop production. In order to understand the extent to which the chosen villages are representative of these farming systems it is first necessary to consider their position within the agrarian structures of the country as a whole.

Crop production in the Sudan can be divided into three sub-sectors covering irrigated, mechanised and traditional farming systems. Table 2.1 shows that while the irrigated sub-sector accounted for only 18.5 per cent of the total area under cultivation in 1973/74 - 1975/76, it contributed more than half the total production of major crops. This contrasts sharply with the substantially larger land area under mechanised agriculture (37 per

Table 2.1: Percentage share of different production sectors
            in area and production of major crops

Production sector	3 years average 1973/74 - 1975/76	
	Area	Production
Irrigated	18.5	50.3
Mechanised	37.2	35.4
Traditional	44.3	14.3
Total	100.0	100.0

Source: Adapted from Six Year Plan 1977/78 - 1982/83, Vol. 2, Table
         6, p. 20.

cent of the total area cultivated) which, however, represented only 35
per cent of production due to significantly lower productivity. About
80 per cent of the mechanised farms are in the Eastern region, with
the rest in Habila in Southern Kordofan. Perhaps the most striking
point to emerge from the table concerns the traditional agricultural
sub-sector: while approximately 80 per cent of the rural population
(about 11.5 million people) depended for their livelihood on
traditional agriculture, they controlled only 44.3 per cent of the
total land area under major crops (about 4.25 million feddans) and
contributed only 14.3 per cent of production.

Out of a total of 80.1 million feddans of land in the Eastern
region, only 3.6 million were cultivated in 1981 (table 2.2). Of
these, roughly 3 million feddans were cultivated by a total of 1,005
registered farmers with mechanised schemes while the remaining 0.6
million were distributed among the rest of the rural population.
Given a total population of 1.2 million in the region where 94 per
cent of the working population was engaged in agricultural activities
in 1964-65[1] it is evident that the Eastern region is marked by very
striking inequalities in landholding.

Table 2.2:   Land area in the eastern region

Land type	Area (million feddans)
Cultivated	3.6
Non-arable	34.0
Pastures	43.4
Total	80.1

Source: Ministry of Agriculture, Agricultural
Statistics 1981.

The major part of the cultivated area in the Eastern region lies within the 600 - 700 mm isohyts. This low total rainfall is, however, subject to substantial seasonal and annual variation which makes farming a precarious way of life. In the rainfed areas dura is the most widespread crop. Little sesame or cotton is grown in the Gedaref area while these crops are grown on a larger scale in the Damazine area of the former Blue Nile province where rainfall levels are higher. Some vegetables are grown in the region for home consumption and the market on gereif land where the river flood ensures an additional and more reliable water supply.

Mechanised rainfed agriculture

Mechanised farming was introduced in the Eastern region in 1944 as part of the British colonial administration's policy of promoting export food crops for countries in the British sphere of influence. The original scheme involved the establishment of a state farm in the Gadambaliya district where the ploughing and threshing of dura was mechanised. However, since labour for weeding and harvesting had to be hired at official government rates, the high labour costs and low crop yields and prices resulted in the scheme's financial failure. In 1948 a tenancy system based on 28-feddan plots and a fifty-fifty sharecropping arrangement was introduced for smallholders. However, this semi-mechanised scheme also foundered for a number of reasons,[2] the most critical of which was low yields which made it impossible to cover the mechanisation costs. In 1954 the current system of large-scale mechanised farming was established, based on 1,000 or 1,500 feddan production units for which tenants pay only a nominal rent of 25 piastres per feddan per year. These large schemes attracted merchants from Gedaref, Khartoum and the Northern province who had capital to invest as well as retired government officials, all of whom had access to credit. On average, mechanised farmers cultivate three schemes each, although there are apparently substantial numbers who farm between 10,000 - 35,000 feddans.

The state-run Mechanised Farming Corporation (MFC) provides a number of important supporting services which include carrying out soil surveys, demarcating and allocating schemes; providing agricultural services (extension, research, seeds and other production inputs, maintenance of agricultural machinery, supervision of the distribution of fuel and spare parts, reporting of pest outbreaks to the crop protection department); representation of local farmers' opinions on such matters as prices and export policy to the relevant government authorities; and finally co-ordination with other government departments to meet these objectives.

Approximately 70 per cent of the 3 million feddans cultivated in the Eastern region are undemarcated: that is, farmers themselves cleared and extended cultivation into uncropped land. This has encroached on the pasture land, leading to disputes with nomads over grazing rights and access to water points and transhumance routes. Since the early 1970s farmers with undemarcated land have also been charged the nominal rent. In 1981 this was increased from 10 piastres per feddan to 25 piastres but despite the increase the MFC is heavily in deficit. The original proposal from government had been a new rate of £S1 per feddan but this was successfully resisted by the powerful Farmers' Union which represents the farmers' interests on matters of government policy and administration in such areas as fuel and spare

parts allocation and distribution, pricing, marketing, taxation and
land rents. The mechanised sector accounts for the major part of <u>dura</u>
and sesame exports. While the exact figures for the Eastern region
are not available, their approximate magnitude can be appreciated from
the fact that in 1973 the total volume of sesame exports was 122,000
tons compared with 110,000 tons of coarse grains consisting mainly of
sorghum.[3] The large expansion of mechanised agriculture in the last
ten years would undoubtedly have produced a correspondingly
significant increase in exports, despite some fluctuations due to
erratic climatic conditions.

Traditional farming sub-sector

The average size of farms in this sub-sector is small, varying
between about 2 to 20 <u>feddans</u>. The main staple crop is <u>dura</u>, in
addition to which some millet, groundnuts, sesame and vegetables may
also be grown. While most of the production is destined for household
consumption, small quantities are also marketed. As will be indicated
later, farm incomes are generally very low and have to be supplemented
by wage employment, trading or crafts and trades such as
blacksmithing, carpentry, tailoring or hut building. In the survey
villages there was very little evidence of seasonal migration to urban
areas. If rural-urban migration takes place it is usually permanent
and the migrants are no longer considered part of the rural
communities even if they do send remittances to needy relatives.

All land in the Sudan belongs to the State. In the indigenous
land tenure system, land was communally held by kinship groups, the
members of which had the right to use land for crop production or
pastoralism according to their needs and capacity. This system is now
disintegrating under the pressures of increasing monetisation of the
economy and privatisation of resources. As a result, the majority of
the farmers interviewed in the survey considered that they owned the
land they cultivated, and while they recognised prohibitions on the
renting or sale of land, their heirs would inherit these ownership
rights.

Population movements

Since the end of the last century, Eastern Sudan has been subject to large-scale population movements, both permanent and temporary. These have profoundly altered the distribution of resources and patterns of agricultural production which has in turn resulted in new and different forms of labour demand and use. The three survey villages are representative of these different upheavals which can be summarised as:

(a) The settlement of immigrants from other parts of the Sudan and West Africa displaced by tribal, civil and colonial wars or the enforcement of colonial political and military power (for example, the Taisha and Fellata in Mereibia).

(b) The settlement of some nomadic tribes already living in the area and their increased involvement in sedentary agricultural production (for example, the Dabain of Rawashda).

(c) Government intervention from 1944 onwards to promote mechanised farming on hitherto unused land.

(d) The phenomenon of seasonal migrant agricultural labour created by the rapid growth in demand for labour on the mechanised farming schemes and structural factors in the economies of the sending areas.

(e) The influx of Ethiopian and Eritrean refugees which started as early as the mid-1960s and has considerably increased during the 1970s and early 1980s

The importance of these population movements and the implications for the distribution of resources in the area should emerge more clearly in the following brief profiles of the survey villages and the later discussion of socio-economic differentiation.

Mereibia

The village was founded at the end of the last century by Taisha (a tribe which originates in Eastern Sudan) who had taken part in the Mahdi's Ethiopian campaign. After the recapture of Khartoum by the colonial army in 1899, they were joined by other fleeing Taisha. They organised themselves into two shiakhas and derived their subsistence from the shifting cultivation of millet and dura (sorghum).

However, the Mereibia of today is predominantly a Fellata village. (The term Fellata is a generic name for Fulani, Hausa and other immigrants who fled from the violent imposition of political and military rule by the British and French colonial governments in Nigeria and other West African states such as Mali around the turn of the last century.) Originally settled on the eastern bank of the Atbara river, they moved to Mereibia in the early 1930s. Benefiting from the suspicious and unfavourable attitude of the colonial authorities towards the Taisha, the Fellata's shiakha took over the political leadership of the village which it has maintained ever since. This proved to have important economic implications for the distribution of new resources and economic opportunities. Most of the valuable gereif land created by the construction of the Khashm El Girba dam in 1961 was divided between Fellata households. Permits needed to open roadside shops and cafés after the nearby portion of the Khartoum-Port Sudan road was asphalted in 1980-81 were also given almost exclusively to the Fellata.

Rawashda

The main inhabitants of the village are the Dabaina who claim descent from the Bani Zibian tribe of the Arabian Peninsula. Originally a nomadic camel herding tribe, Rawashda was established early this century as a satellite village for rainy season dura cultivation. In the late 1950s some of the wealthy livestock-owning households got involved in large-scale mechanised dura farming in that area. By 1964 they were so well established in sedentary agriculture that they invested in the provision of a year-round water supply and gave up nomadic herding.

Gadambaliya

The village developed rapidly from 1948 onwards when the mechanised farming tenancy system was initiated for smallholders. A number of households from nomadic tribes such as the Gaali, Rikabia, Arakien and Kenana which had farming satellite villages in the are joined the scheme and moved to Gadambaliya. Also a few Bilala households (a tribe from Chad) were given plots of land.

After the failure of this scheme and the introduction of large-scale mechanised farming schemes, Gadambaliya was allotted 6,000 feddans to distribute between all the households in the village. Twenty-feddan plots were assigned to household heads and in the rare cases where women or male dependants asked for their own land, they were either given a small plot of their own or a portion of the plot assigned to the household head.

Over the years numerous households belonging to various Western Sudanese and Chadian tribes settled in Gadambaliya. Coming first as labourers, (after a year or two) they received a plot of land to cultivate. This resulted in the development of two distinct parts of the village. The old part, where the first settlers live, is predominantly Rikabi while the newer part, one kilometre down the road, is comprised of eight different shiakhas composed of tribes like the Bilala, Mima, Fur, Masaleet, Tama and Dajo as well as some other smaller tribes.

Socio-economic differentiation

Table 2.3 shows the very low absolute levels of household incomes in the three survey villages: 86 per cent of households in both Mereibia and Gadambaliya and 73 per cent in Rawashda have annual

Table 2.3: Percentage distribution of total household income by village, 1981

Income group (£S)	Mereibia	Rawashda	Gadambaliya
< 500	12	1	14
500 - 1 499	50	27	38
1 500 - 2 999	24	45	34
3 000 - 9 999	9	21	11
10 000 - 19 999	5	2	2
20 000 +	0	4	1
TOTAL	100	100	100

Table 2.4: Percentage distribution of households by income group and village, 1981

Income group[a]	Mereibia	Rawashda	Gadambaliya	Total
Rich	5	7	3	5
Medium	33	65	45	48
Poor	62	28	52	47
TOTAL	100	100	100	100

(a) Total annual household income for these groups are:

    Rich   =   £S10,000; Medium = £S1,500 - 9,999;
    Poor   =   £S1,500.

incomes of under £S3,000. This contrasts sharply with the small
percentage of households in each village, and most notably in
Rawashda, which have substantial incomes of over £S10,000 a year.

The disparity in income distribution within and beteween the
villages shows up more strikingly in table 2.4 where we have divided
households into rich, medium and poor-income groups. Significantly
larger numbers of households fall into the medium and rich categories
in Rawashda while Mereibia has the poorest income profile.
Surprisingly there was little difference in average income between the
Fellata and Taisha tribes in Mereibia despite the fact that the
Fellata own 290 per cent more gereif land and 122 per cent more bildat
land (small- to medium-sized holdings of rainfed cropped land).
However, in Gadambaliya tribes from Western Sudan and Chad represented
62 per cent of the households in the poor-income category and none of
the rich. Since many of these settled relatively recently after land
pressure had grown acute in the village, quite a number are landless
while others have significantly less land than the other tribes.

The 29 female-headed households represented a particularly
disadvantaged group: 86 per cent fell in the poor-income group while
the remaining 14 per cent had an annual income of between £S1,500 and
£S3,000.

The average annual incomes per household and per capita for 1981
(table 2.5) again underline the very considerable disparity between
socio-economic groups. The unusually large figure of £S64,332 for
rich households in Rawashda was inflated by one household in the
sample which had 85 members, a distortion which has been absorbed in
the calculations for the per capita income by adult equivalent.
Nevertheless, the high-income households in all three villages did
have significantly larger household population sizes than the poor
(table 2.6). While this may simply reflect the obligation of
relatively wealthy households in rural areas to provide housing and
food for a larger number of relatives and non-relatives and the
ability of households with more members to earn more income, the table

Table 2.5: Average annual income by household and by adult
equivalent, 1981

Income group	Average household income			Average income per adult equivalent[1] (£S)		
	Mereibia	Rawashda	Gadambaliya	Mereibia	Rawashda	Gadambaliya
Rich	11 595	64 332	17 048	1 360	3 383	2 037
Medium	2 945	3 160	2 784	390	501	500
Poor	890	1 094	708	256	312	179

[1] See Appendix Table 1

Table 2.6: Average household population size by income group
and by village, 1981

Income group	Mereibia	Rawashda	Gadambaliya
Rich	11.0	27.7	9.5
Medium	10.5	9.6	8.3
Poor	5.5	5.9	6.6

also raises a more fundamental question about the nature of the
relationship between household population size and the factors
determining the distribution and use of resources.

Although theoretically Eastern Sudan has abundant land, in
practice there is considerable pressure on land within convenient
walking distance from the villages. Thus a substantial proportion of
households in the survey villages had little or no village land (table
2.7). When they also had few other productive assets they found it
difficult to finance the cultivation of land further away (which would

at least require investment in transport) or engage in other reasonably remunerative income-generating activites. The inevitable result would be poverty and the inability to support many people, thereby forcing some of the able-bodied members to migrate or to search for other wage employment.

Table 2.7: Percentage distribution of land by village, 1981

Feddans[1]	Mereibia	Rawashda	Gadambaliya
0	1	6	6
< 10	30	7	16
10 - 49	56	53	66
50 - 99	7	17	3
100 - 499	5	10	5
500 +	1	7	4
Totals	100	100	100

[1] 1 feddan = 1.04 acres or 0.42 hectares.

In contrast, households with large resource endowments may well resist possible opportunities to subdivide the property according to inheritance rights, an act which would lead to the formation of a number of smaller households. The pooling of earned and inherited resources would be to everyone's mutual financial advantage since it would enable them to undertake jointly large-scale enterprises which would bring higher net returns per unit of capital than the individual partners could make alone. This type of large. rich household is characteristic of the extended family structures of the nomadic tribes since a herd must have a certain minimum size to be economically viable and for the households as a whole to ensure political and personal security in what are generally adverse conditions. The rich households of Rawashda and Gadambaliya are all settled nomads who still maintain this form of family organisation which, as we point out in the next section, proved to be a major factor in enabling them to accumulate the resources necessary to engage in large-scale mechanised farming.

Table 2.8: Percentage distribution of land by income group, 1981

Income group	Feddans				
	0	50	50-99	100-499	500+
Rich	0	1	4	11	69
Medium	38	45	76	63	31
Poor	62	54	20	26	0
Totals	100	100	100	100	100

Structural factors underlying the distribution of resources

Enormous disparities in both the absolute value of assets and the distribution of land and other productive assets between income groups emerge very strikingly in tables 2.6 and 2.9. While the rich-income category represents only 5 per cent of the sample households, it accounts for 74 per cent of total assets. This contrasts sharply with the medium-income households (48 per cent of the sample) which own 22 per cent of total assets while the poorest group, representing 47 per cent of the sample households, have only 4 per cent. These dramatic figures suggest that there are structural factors underlying these vast disparities of wealth between the rich and poor which lead essentially to the existence of two quite distinct types of rainfed agricultural production systems in Eastern Sudan: small-holder and large-scale mechanised farming.

Table 2.9: Average value of household assets by income group, 1981 (£S)

Income group	Agricultural	Livestock	Shops/cafes	Trucks/cars	Non-farm machinery	Consumer	Financial	Total
Rich	23,993	6,994	2,154	14,144	1,651	10,893	215	60,044
Medium	4,180	841	291	44	29	38	10	5,433
Poor	12	243	20	0	7	11	0.5	293.5

The basic differentiating factor arises from the fact that in both systems the cultivation of the major crop, dura, is characterised by low inputs and low yields. Since at present no satisfactory high-yielding dura varieties with good fertilizer response rates exist, it is almost impossible to raise productivity per unit area to levels which would significantly improve financial returns. The only way to increase total income is to expand very substantially the area under cultivation. This, however, implies a new mode of production involving the commercialisation of agriculture which makes mechanisation and the hiring of labour possible.

The poor are caught in an impasse. Since productivity levels are so low, it is impossible to save enough out of traditional agriculture to move into commercial production. All the commercial farmers interviewed in Gedaref and the survey villages had first accumulated their capital in non-farming enterprises. The most numerous group were wealthy traders, including grain merchants, who vertically integrated into large-scale dura production in the 1950s onwards. As part of the Gedaref business community, they had easy access to bank loans and sheil (a form of crop mortgage) to finance operating costs. It is worth noting, however, that the wealthiest people in Gedaref are not farmers (an occupation they consider too risky in the unreliable climatic conditions of Eastern Sudan) but are involved in large-scale trading, grain storage and exporting, and sheil.

There are two distinct forms of sheil. The first one takes the
form of the borrower purchasing dura from the lender on the basis of
deferred payment at prices 30 - 50 per cent higher than the spot
market prices. Once contracts (which usually include collateral in
the form of a post-dated cheque or property) are signed, the borrower
transports the grains from the lender's stores and sells at the spot
price. This type of borrowing is practised by farmers who do not have
the needed working capital and it is usually done before the beginning
of the season (May) or during the weeding (August). Repayment takes
place at the end of the season (January) in cash or grain equivalent.

The second type of sheil is a simple variation of forward
contracting usually required to cover harvest and post-harvest costs.
The borrower goes long and the lender short at very low future prices
(40 to 60 per cent). Payment of the total value of the transaction is
received in cash after signing the contract (September - October) and
the borrower is obliged to deliver the purchased crop to the lender's
stores on a specific date at the end of the season (January).

Another important source of finance for mechanised farming
schemes is the sale of livestock. This is typified by the rich
households in Rawashda and Gadambaliya. Originally nomadic herders
with large households, they pooled their livestock assets and invested
heavily in large-scale farming. While the poor hold 83 per cent of
their total assets in the form of livestock and only 4 per cent in
agricultural assets, about 12 per cent of the assets of the rich are
held in livestock and 40 per cent in agricultural assets. This
suggests a substantial transformation of wealth accumulated in the
nomadic mode into productive agricultural assets. Subsequently these
settled nomads have vertically integrated their commercial farming
enterprises, incorporating trading and road transport businesses.

A third form of capital accumulation observed particularly in
Mereibia was the road-side café serving the heavy lorry and other
traffic on the Khartoum - Port Sudan road. Only set up in the early
1980s after this section of the road was asphalted, these cafés are

making substantial profits which their owners are now beginning to
re-invest in commercial agriculture.

These substantial disparities in wealth lead to the development
and maintenance of two distinct but inter-dependent farming systems.
These differ essentially in the scale of operation and the heavy
reliance of mechanised farming on hired labour which is drawn from the
traditional farming sector (both local and Sudanese migrant labour)
and from among the refugee population.

III. Strategies of labour use

This section examines the labour strategies of the different
socio-economic categories discussed earlier and the implications for
the operation of a rural labour market. Here we take the household as
the basic unit of analysis, emphasising nonetheless the complex set of
rights and obligations regarding labour use and the access to, and
control of, resources and income exercised by different members of the
household. Not only do the norms for different ethnic and
socio-economic groups vary according to gender, age and skills but
also actual practices are being modified as the result of expanding
opportunities for education and non-farm employment and increased
population pressure on limited resources. Both undermine the
authority of village elders and household heads and therefore their
control over the labour of young dependents.

The mix of labour strategies of different household members
depends on the value and diversity of resources, the degree of
autonomy of individuals, the need for collective labour to ensure
survival or to enhance profits or, conversely, the need for a variety
of different sources of employment and income to spread risks and
thereby to improve the security of the household unit. A labour
strategy offers three basic choices:

(a) how much household or individual labour to allocate to
     exploiting household and/or personal land, other capital
     assets and skills;

(b)   how much household or individual labour to sell (i.e. hire out);

(c)   how much and what type of labour to hire in.

Several combinations of these aspects of labour strategy are possible. A household or an individual may hire and sell the same type of labour over time according to the availability of, or need for, cash. Or one member of a household may sell labour at the same time that another member is hiring the same type of labour, depending on their autonomy. Another possible combination is that of hiring one type of labour (for example, unskilled) and selling another type, specialised in some skill. Finally, some people may hire in labour, using their own labour for supervision; while others might only have labour to sell.

These different combinations of labour use and the ways in which they are exchanged both within and outside the labour market are affected by four factors: the resource base of different socio-economic groups; the division of labour within the household; the seasonal nature of agricultural work and its integration with non-farm occupations; and, lastly, trends and changes over time in the relative incidence and importance of market and non-market contracts. These are discussed in more detail below.

(a)   The resource base of different socio-economic groups

Appendix tables A2 and A3, giving the distribution of different occupations among the adult population (defined as those aged 15 and above) for the three broad income categories in the survey villages, throw light on the relationship between the resource base and the choice of occupation. While farming was the major occupation in all categories, it is significant that it declined as a proportion of all occupations from a high of 50 per cent of men and 21 per cent of women in the poor category to only 29 per cent of men and 4 per cent of women in the rich category. This, together with the distribution of other occupations, suggests that the rich, who are better endowed with land and other capital assets, have relatively greater opportunities to diversify and to invest in non-farm businesses such as trading and cafés. Several of the rich households own tractors and trucks which also provide employment as drivers for some of their members.

The medium income group contains the majority of the own-account traders and café owners who also require some capital, as well as most of the herders who tend their own livestock (the rich are more likely to hire herders). The non-farming occupations of the poor are predominantly those which require little capital such as petty trading, tailoring and crafts (blacksmith, carpenter, potter, painter, bricklayer, plumber, leather worker) or consist in selling unskilled or skilled manual labour for such work as farm and non-farm labouring and hut building.

Apart from farming and domestic work, the main occupations performed by women of the medium- and low-income groups (few women among the rich are engaged in income-earning activities) are brewing, mat and basket making, and the preparation and selling of cooked foods.

Finally, the distribution of young men and women aged 15 and above in higher education and training clearly reflects the greater ease with which the richer groups can release their labour to allow them to continue in full-time education. Not surprisingly, women represented only 17 per cent of those benefiting from higher education. This skewed access to higher education and training will only serve to reinforce existing inequalities between socio-economic groups and between men and women.

(b) The division of labour within the household according to gender and age. This varies with different tribes and with the socio-economic status of households, and is affected by inheritance practices and other customs which determines the ownership and control of resources and income.

Lahoween, Bilala and Taisha women living in the Eastern region may inherit, own and cultivate land and then dispose of the crop. Women of the other tribes living in the three survey villages may be explicitly denied inheritance rights to land; or else their brothers are customarily allowed to use the land in return for a small gift (in theory at least). The women of these tribes are not supposed to work in the fields although, as table 2.10 shows, in poor and medium-income households many are invariably forced to do so.

Table 2.10: Percentage of women engaged in income-generating activities

Income group	Per cent
Rich	16
Medium	30
Poor	50

This table is particularly striking in view of the commonly quoted female activity rate in Kassala province of only 6 per cent (Agricultural Census 1964-65). This discrepancy may be explained by the fact that male household heads in this area feel that they lose status if their wives are involved in agricultural and other income-earning work. We were able to detect that, in the case of agricultural work at least, many of the respondents denied or grossly underestimated the incidence and amount of female labour. This was particularly noticeable in the case of home threshing of dura, and, more importantly, the weeding, picking and drying of vegetables from the gereif land. This under-reporting inevitably leads to the invisibility of women's labour and an under-estimation of their actual economic roles.

Employment opportunities for male dependents such as younger brothers and sons also vary considerably between socio-economic groups and tribes. However, in contrast to women, if they feel the household head exercises an unacceptable degree of control over their labour and household resources, they can leave and set up their own households. This tends to happen fairly easily in poor households where the few resources are generally controlled and utilised by the household head; younger men will be forced to sell their labour and may have to migrate to find work. In contrast, if the head of a rich household dies, his successor may try to prevent the actual division of the property between the heirs to exploit fully the potential for investment and employment creation that substantial capital resources bring. There was one particularly notable example of a wealthy household with 85 members in one of the survey villages where this type of extended family enterprise was very successful. All the adult men were responsible for one aspect of the joint business and appeared to be considerably more wealthy than they would have been had the household disintegrated into its sub-units. However, in many cases men dislike their position of social and economic dependence on the household head and prefer to take their share of household property and establish their own households. This indicates that men have a greater degree of socially sanctioned control over resources and their own labour, than women, for women do not have this option of founding independent homes in rural areas (female household heads are generally widows).

(c) <u>The seasonality of work in rainfed agriculture</u> and the precarious returns in areas of unreliable rainfall and poor soil as in the Eastern region makes it imperative that men and women have other income-generating ocupations in the slack periods. Table 2.11 demonstrates clearly that in the poor-income group 60 per cent of the adult men and 33 per cent of the women have more than one occupation, thereby spreading risks but unfortunately only ensuring a meagre survival. Even nearly a third of the rich farmers and traders increase their wealth and security by diversifying into at least two occupations.

Table 2.11: Percentage of working population with two or three occupations by gender

Income group	2 occupations		3 occupations	
	Male	Female	Male	Female
Rich	29	8	5	0
Medium	57	20	7	2
Poor	60	33	9	6

(d) Trends in market and non-market labour contracts. The phasing out of slave labour in agriculture (for example, among the Fellata and Lahoween in the east) brought about a parallel increase in the use of both unpaid family labour among the freeborn and communal labour groups (nafirs) to fill the resulting shortfall in labour supply. However, the predominance of these forms of non-market labour has been undermined in recent years, partly as the result of the declining authority of village elders and household heads who now experience greater difficulty in controlling the labour of the village youth as well as their own dependents, and partly because of the growing employment opportunities in the cash economies of Sudan and the Gulf States. Competition with wage labouring jobs was brought closer to home within the Eastern region itself with the rapid and large-scale expansion of mechanised farming schemes in the 1950s onwards, creating a substantial demand for paid labour. This has resulted in the increasing monetisation of intra-village agricultural labour, with wage rates forced up to levels similar to those paid on the large farms. Since most of the wage-earning opportunities occur in the male-classified jobs, female labour remains largely unmonetised.

Table 2.12 shows that for the rich-income group the major sources of income are the mechanised farming tenancies, supplemented by trading. Although the primary occupation of the poorer groups is

also farming, the low net returns have compelled the majority to
diversify into other occupations, particularly wage employment and
their own businesses such as trading or tailoring. The average annual
incomes of a variety of these occupations are given in Appendix
table A4.

Table 2.12: Percentage distribution of income components by income group

Income group	Agriculture	Livestock sales	Wages	Trading/ own businesses	Remittances	Zakat	Other	Total
Poor	49	1	21	10	12	6	1	100
Medium	42	6	25	22	1	1	3	100
Rich	60	4	4	25	1	0	6	100

The poorest group receive as much as 18 per cent of their total
income in gifts, in the form of remittances or zakat, which underlines
the importance of these social mechanisms for income redistribution.
The remittances suggest that poverty is a major force behind migrant
labour in this group while the rich are considerably more likely to be
able to provide employment for their relatives at home.

Almost all the mechanised farming schemes in the Gedaref area
mono-crop dura while farms further south in the higher rainfall belt
rotate dura and sesame. Although the major food and cash crop on the
smaller bildat farms is also dura, there is some rotation and
inter-cropping in the Gedaref area with millet and the legume lubia
(Dolichos Lablab). A variety of vegetables (onions, okra, tomatoes,
aubergine, cucumbers and water melon) are grown on the gereif land for
both home consumption and sale.

Gereif land is cultivated between January and May, planting taking place as soon as the river flood recedes sometime in January. Since the river refloods in June and July as the rainy season gets under way, there is no competition for labour between the vegetable and rainfed dura crops.

There are striking variations in the use of labour in rainfed agriculture in Eastern Sudan according to size of landholding units. While the data on socio-economic differentiation discussed in section II indicated a clear distinction between the small-holder traditional farming system on the one hand and large-scale mechanised farming schemes on the other, in fact there is no rigid cut-off point in cultivation practices between these two systems. All farmers use similar agronomic methods. Since breeding programmes still have not produced good high-yielding dura varieties and existing varieties have low fertilizer response rates, farmers have a limited choice of seed varieties which they cultivate without fertilizer. Neither large or small farmers commonly practise crop rotations and fallows are declining throughout the region, due largely to land pressure in the case of the small farmers and the structure of relative costs and returns for the large enterprises.

However, with regard to the use of labour and mechanisation, farms of different sizes appear to be on a continuum. The number of work days required per operation per feddan declines as the size of the landholding expands (table 2.13) and this decline is inversely related to the increases use of mechanised techniques (table 2.14). Even small-holders rely fairly heavily on mechanised land preparation and planting to expand the area under cultivation and ensure timely sowing since this has a critical effect on yields. Since land preparation and threshing are also the most strenuous operation, their mechanisation is particularly attractive to farmers.

The participation of household women and children in agricultural work increases substantially as the size of landholding falls (Table 2.15). This could be explained by the fact that the small-holders,

- 47 -

Table 2.13: Average number of workdays per feddan by cultural operation and holding size, 1981

	Average number of workdays				
Holding size feddans	Land preparation and planting	Weeding	Harvesting	Threshing	Totals
< 10	2.8	4.1	2.1	1.3	10.3
10- 19	1.3	3.3	2.1	1.2	7.9
20- 49	0.6	2.1	1.8	1.0	5.5
50-99	0.1	1.6	1.8	1.2	4.7
100-499	0.06	2.1	1.6	0.5	4.26
500+	0.02	2.2	1.5	0.1	3.82

Table 2.14: Percentage of farms with mechanised land preparation, planting and threshing of dura by holding size

Holding size feddans	Land preparation/ planting	Threshing
< 10	42	15
10- 19	70	35
20- 49	88	38
50- 99	94	17
100-499	88	63
500+	100	80

Table 2.15: Percentage distribution of male, female and
child household agricultural labour by holding size

Holding size feddans	Household agricultural labour			
	Male	Female	Child	Total
< 10	54	40	6	100
10- 19	70	18	12	100
20- 49	73	17	10	100
50- 99	63	16	21	100
100-499	94	3	3	100
500+	90	9	1	100

who are in the poor-income group, also have the smallest household
population sizes (and therefore workforces) and so have to draw on all
available labour. However, two other explanations are also likely.
First, as we saw in the previous section, insufficient land forces the
majority of the poorest male farmers into taking secondary, non-farm
employment which in turn necessitates the women taking over some of
the farming work in addition to their other tasks. Second, quite a
number of Taisha women in Mereibia and Bilala women in Gadambaliya
owned small plots of land which they cultivated on their own account.

Indeed, the role of women in agriculture varied significantly
between villages. In Gadambaliya women accounted for 28 per cent of
total household agricultural labour, compared with 12 per cent in
Mereibia and only 2 per cent in Rawashda. While these disparities
might be partly explained by tribal differences, the use of female
agricultural labour is inversely related to household income levels.
Since the latter were significantly higher in Rawashda it is not
surprising that female participation in farming is correspondingly
lower.

What is, however, surprising is the high percentage of small-holder households with under 20 _feddans_ hiring labour 'for weeding, harvesting and threshing (table 2.16). There are three possible explanations. First, the household may simply have insufficient labour available and may be forced to supplement household with hired labour. Second, the farmers may calculate that they get higher net returns if they take on alternative wage or own-account employment and hire agricultural labour. The third reason stems from the very noticeable phenomenon (from the questionnaire survey as well as general observations in the villages) of numerous young men who did little farm or herding work but expected to eat from the family pot. The result of increased aspirations on the part of the (often semi-educated) young men, combined with a disdain for hard manual work and the declining authority of household and village elders, this is beginning to become a relatively serious social problem. The immediate consequence is harder work for the male elders and the women and greater pressure on scarce financial resources to hire farm labour. Mereibia farmers are also increasingly relying on Hadendawa herders to look after their cattle. The implications for the young men themselves are less clear given the difficulty of finding reasonably remunerative work for the semi-educated and semi-skilled.

Table 2.16:   Percentage of households hiring labour for weeding, harvesting and threshing dura by holding size

Holding size feddans	Weeding	Harvesting	Threshing
< 10	6	11	7
10- 19	29	40	27
20- 49	63	67	39
50- 99	83	83	67
100-499	100	100	38
500+	100	100	100

The need to pay labour in advance of marketing the crops poses a serious problem for many farmers. Large farmers with schemes finance these operations through bank loans or sheil. However, the Agricultural Bank and the commercial banks generally only make advances to individuals or co-operatives with at least 1,000 feddans. For the small farmers with very low net returns the sheil system is particularly onerous, all the more so when unreliable rains or sudden pests can result in partial or total crop failure. Some small farmers try to circumvent these dangers by selling the crops - particularly the gereif vegetable crop - in advance. The purchaser is then responsible for the labour (sometimes hiring the landowner himself) and, more importantly, the risks involved.

Despite the similarities in cultivation practices, it is nonetheless evident that there are two distinct farming systems, differentiated essentially by scale of operation and absolute size of net returns. The two, however, are inter-dependent since the large-scale mechanised system relies on labour provided by the poor traditional farmers. Returns in the subsistence sector are so low that households are forced to supplement agricultural production with wage employment or own-account businesses.

In the Eastern region as a whole, where mechanised farming schemes cover about 3 million out of 3.6 million feddans, the demand for labour for weeding (the period of peak demand) is roughly 3 million x 2.2 workdays per feddan (see table 2.13), giving a total of 6.6 million workdays over a period of four months. Clearly the traditional agricultural sector in the Eastern region is incapable of meeting such a massive demand. However, the comparative poverty of subsistence farming households in the West and South of Sudan created a migrant labour force which filled the gap between supply and demand for agricultural wage labour. Since the 1960s the influx of refugees from Eritrea and other parts of Ethiopia into the Eastern region has substantially increased the supply of labour available locally. The implications of this for the migrant labourers and the whole question of the supply and demand of seasonal agricultural labour are discussed in the following sub-section.

The demand for and supply of labour

There are two aspects to the problem: the question of overall demand and supply of labour and that of the differential demand and supply of labour for different crops and operations. In the mid-1970s many commercial farmers were complaining of general labour shortages and high labour costs, presumably to justify investment in further mechanisation which would entail high costs in terms of foreign exchange. It was argued that reported rises in wage rates over a number of years reflected a limited supply of labour. However, this is not a necessary nor a convincing conclusion for three reasons. First, one would expect some wage increases over time to compensate for inflation. Unfortunately, this is difficult to substantiate in practice given the basic problem of estimating real wage increases since no reliable time series date of wage rates nor indices of inflation for the same time periods are available for rural areas.

The second reason why rises in wage rates do not necessarily imply labour shortages and could equally be compatible with a labour surplus, is that we are far from a situation of perfect competition. The irregularity of the work and the individual bargain made for each contract could lead to labourers demanding high wages on which they could subsist during possible subsequent periods of unemployment. At the same time farmers are constrained by critical time limits on agricultural operations which limit their bargaining power.

Thirdly, if there really were a situation of serious labour shortage one would have expected the labourers to have insisted on daily wage payments based on a fixed number of hours, rather than the existing system of team tasks or piece work contracts which result in their working from sunrise to sunset. The prevailing task system is clearly to the farmers' advantage and reflects their stronger bargaining position as they have almost no supervision costs and they can count on group pressure on the individual to maintain high work standards.

An earlier study examined the question of labour supply and demand and labour costs in some detail for the irrigated sector in Kassala and the former Blue Nile provinces (though the issues are similar for mechanised rainfed agriculture) and concluded that while labour was in short supply at certain periods there was no absolute labour shortage and that "more labour would be forthcoming at somewhat higher wages and somewhat higher recruitment costs".[4]

By the time of our survey in 1982 the situation in the Eastern region, at least, had changed and there appeared to be a labour surplus even during the peak period of dura weeding. A number of farmers recalled that in the past there had been a labour shortage and they had to hire contractors to recruit and transport labourers from the West and South of the country. They had also to offer the enticement of a wage advance. However, they stated that the growing refugee influx from the late 1970s onwards had created a large local labour force which had almost eliminated their former dependence on contractors.

It is not known whether the decline in the role of the contractors brought about a parallel decline in the number of migrants coming from the South and West. The supply of migrants might have fallen off because of competition from refugees. It is also possible that the substantial increase in labour available locally had the effect of reducing wages or at least holding them constant despite inflationary pressures. This would have made migration to the East for casual agricultural labouring jobs less attractive. At the same time mechanised farming was expanding in Habila in Southern Kordofan but there is no evidence as to whether former migrants to the East now go to Habila or whether the proximity of Habila has attracted different types of labourers, including women who might not be able to venture as far as the East. Unfortunately the absence of time series data on real wage rates in Habila and in the Eastern and Central regions makes it impossible to do more than make plausible guesses about changes and trends in the supply of migrant and refugee labour.

It is clearly difficult to estimate the size of the reported labour surplus occurring in recent years in the Eastern region. Certainly it fluctuates from year to year, not only because of factors affecting supply but perhaps more importantly due to variations in demand. This was particularly apparent in 1982 when the unusually late start of the rains led to a fall in the area under dura from over 3 million feddans in 1981 to an estimated 2.9 million in 1982, with a consequent drop in labour demand. At the same time the poor rains are likely to have increased the number of people looking for labouring jobs to compensate for their own inadequate or failed crops.

The effects of the reduction in labour demand and the resulting labour surplus were striking. There was a fall in nominal wage rates despite high and continuing inflation (table 2.17) implying a greater fall in real wages. The average length of time labourers remained unemployed during the peak period of labour demand for weeding is unfortunately underestimated in table 2.18. Many of the scores of labourers sitting on the pavements waiting for work opportunities were suspicious (despite our denials) that we might pass on information to the police and consequently refused to be interviewed. Hearing this, several commercial farmers gave us permission to interview labourers in their offices when the latter came for payment. These labourers, fresh from work, with money in their pockets and not yet depressed by unemployment, were considerably more ready to take part in the survey. Unfortunately, however, this inevitably biased negatively our estimates of the periods of time labourers were unemployed by exaggerating the proportion of people unemployed for only a day rather than longer. Nonetheless, the table indicates that, on the conservative side, more than 30 per cent had been unemployed for more than a week at the peak period of demand.

Evidence for a differential demand and supply of labour for different crops and cultural operations also emerged from table 2.17. That the period of peak labour demand occurs with sesame and dura weeding[5] is reflected in higher wages paid for these operations. The figures for gum arabic harvesting may be underestimated, partly due to the small number of respondents doing

Table 2.17: Average daily cash wages by crop

		Average daily wage (£S)	
Crop	Operation	1981	1982
Dura	Weeding	6.02	5.80
Dura	Harvesting	5.13	n.a.
Sesame	Weeding	6.10	4.73
Sesame	Harvesting	5.05	n.a.
Cotton	Harvesting	4.88	n.a.
Gum Arabic	Harvesting	3.76	n.a.

skilled operation

this work. Gum arabic harvesting is a skilled operation most commonly carried out by migrants from Kordofan who come east after their dura harvest. Since our survey took place in September-October we would not, therefore, have encountered many representatives of this category of worker.

The highest paid labourers on the dura crop are the threshers, another category of specialised workers whom we did not cover in our survey. Also organised as team work, mechanised threshing is generally carried out at night to prevent the machines from over-heating. The 1982 rate of pay was 50 piastres per ardeb for both those feeding the machines and for those filling and sewing the sacks. A team of 11 can manage between 150-350 ardeb a night.

machine feeders!

In practice migrant labour supply responds to income earned over the season rather than to an imputed daily wage rate. Because the nature of demand involves two peak periods for weeding and harvesting, with a slack period in between, employers need to resort to various strategies to ensure adequate labour for the major periods of demand. These form a flexible mix of fluctuations in wage levels, recourse to

Employers Str

labour contractors or labour-saving practices such as reploughing and planting instead of hand weeding if fields become choked with weeds early in the season. This choice of strategies increases the large farmers' room for manoeuvre and therefore their control over the labour market.

IV. Seasonal agricultural labourers

In this section we examine the labour market from the perspective of the seasonal agricultural labourers. Many live locally and have little or no land. However, the majority are either migrants from the West or South of the Sudan or are refugees. Although, as we saw in the last chapter, small to medium farmers hire a considerable amount of labour, the largest sources of employment by far are the mechanised farming schemes which altogether cover about 3 million feddans.

The "stranger" status of the migrants and refugees makes them vulnerable to possible exploitation and raises a series of questions which we examine below on their position in, and degree of control over, labour market processes. What, for example, are the pull and push factors affecting the supply of migrant and refugee labour at present? To what extent would higher wages alone increase the labour supply or are there other social and economic constraints to increasing the labour supply, both absolutely or seasonally? How does the wage bargain operate and to what extent do the conditions under which it takes place expose labourers to possible exploitation, especially since they are not covered by the Labour Laws? Is the remuneration sufficient to cover only the labourers' subsistence requirements or will it also provide the subsistence and reproductive needs of the whole family? What are the implications of migration for wage labour for the migrants' families and the economies of the sending areas? Do women, for example, have to take on the male migrants' work in addition to their own? Is food security threatened? Finally, under what conditions do the labourers work and live, and are these compatible with the current Six Year Plan's stated

ocial equity, full, self-rewarding and productive
This last question is perhaps the most crucial as it
raises fundamental concept of the type of society Sudan is
striving to build and which shapes the objectives and content of its
development strategy.

Regional imbalances and internal labour movement

The Sudan has an unusually high rate of internal labour
migration, estimated at about 1 million workers a year (roughly 14 per
cent of the national labour force). Approximately 800,000 (80 per
cent) are rural-rural migrants.[7] Nearly 50 per cent of all migrants
are from Kordofan and Darfur while Kassala and the former Blue Nile
provinces receive about 40 per cent of the total. These figures
exclude the nomadic livestock herders.

The most important factor affecting this inter-regional migration
and the demand and supply of labour in irrigated and mechanised
rainfed agriculture is the extremely skewed distribution of public and
private investment of both capital and expertise between the modern
and traditional agricultural sectors. During the Five Year Plan,
amended to cover the seven years 1970-77, actual expenditure on
agriculture amounted to £S146.4 million, of which only an
insignificant share was spent in developing the traditional sector.
The Six Year Plan, 1977/78 - 1982/83, states that a major objective is
the "development and modernisation of the traditional agricultural
sector",[8] and yet little of the £S715 million allocated to the
agricultural sector in the Plan period has been earmarked for the
traditional sector.[9] An unspecified amount has been allocated for
surveys and research for developing traditional agriculture but the
only operational investment projects are the Sag El Naam project
(£S2.1 million) and an agricultural development project in the Nuba
Mountains area (£S6.7 million).

This large disparity in investment between the modern and
traditional agricultural sectors is also reflected in extreme regional

imbalances: <u>about 90 per cent of the modern irrigated and mechanised</u> <u>farming schemes are in Kassala and the former Blue Nile provinces</u> (1) <u>while in the west and south of the country, traditional small-holder</u> <u>agricultural predominates.</u> Furthermore, a comparison of all the existing household budget and farm management surveys carried out in different parts of the Sudan indicates that rural household incomes in Kordofan, Darfur and Bahr el Ghazal are significantly lower than in the Eastern and Central regions.[10] <u>To some extent this can be</u> (2) <u>explained by the slightly higher rainfall and better soils in the</u> <u>East.</u> Another factor is the greater population pressure on land in (3) the West which has resulted in reduced fallows and declining yields. <u>This could only be compensated for by</u> intensifying land use and <u>raising productivity through</u> the application of improved seed varieties, fertilizers, pesticides and mechanisation, all of which <u>require</u> substantial <u>cash investment</u> frequently beyond the rsesources of the rural poor. In such a situation many farmers may calculate that they <u>get higher</u> returns for their labour in wage labouring jobs <u>in the east than in</u> cultivating their own land.

At the same time, the development of highly-capitalised irrigated and large-scale mechanised farming mainly in the Eastern and Central regions has required the massive influx of seasonal labourers. Absolute poverty in the west and south, compounded by official disinterest in developing traditional agriculture, the lack of credit and modern production inputs to increase productivity, has thus forced large numbers of the rural poor into migrant agricultural labouring jobs.

Who are the labourers?

In order to examine the questions raised at the beginning of this section on the seasonal agricultural labourers' reasons for engaging in this type of work, and their position in and degree of control over the labour market process, a survey of 265 labourers was carried out in the Gedaref area. As would be expected from the large proportion of Western Sudanese in the national migrant population, just over half of the seasonal labourers interviewed in the survey were born in the Western region (table 2.19). The relatively low number of migrants from Southern Kordofan compared with those from the other parts of the Western region reflects the alternative and more convenient wage-earning opportunities in the Habila mechanised farming scheme in that area.

The refugees from Eritrea and other parts of Ethiopia accounted for 19 per cent of the respondents. It is perhaps worth noting that 43 per cent of them now consider Sudan (the central and particularly the eastern regions) to be their home.

All but one of the respondents were male. While this is consistent with the clear predominance of men in farming in the Kassala province, the almost complete absence of women among the seasonal labourers hired for dura weeding contrasts sharply with the situation in the Habila scheme where women represent about 30 per cent of the casual labour force engaged in dura and sesame weeding and harvesting.[11] To some extent this reflects the relative immobility of women engaged in child care and domestic work who tend to undertake employment nearer home. However, women are engaged in certain agricultural wage labouring tasks in the east. Some refugee and migrant women undertake cotton picking work on irrigation schemes and Bilala women are reputed to be active in sesame harvesting.

Table 2.18: Length of time unemployed during the peak period of labour demand for weeding

Time period	Per cent of unemployed respondents
1 day	31
1 week	38
1 - 4 weeks	18
1 month	13
Total	100

The majority of the respondents were under 30 years of age (table 2.20). Nearly half were household heads, most of whom were married. There was no significant difference in age groups, marital status or numbers of household heads coming from different regions.

Sixty per cent of the respondents were illiterate while 28 per cent could read and write a little and only 12 per cent claimed to read and write well. The refugees had the lowest literacy levels (33 per cent) while the labourers from the Eastern region have the highest levels (58 per cent). Fifty-seven per cent of the respondents had no formal education and only 7 per cent had gone beyond primary school.

The survey did not substantiate the commonly-held view that migrants tend to move between different jobs and areas, in irrigated and mechanised farming schemes, as well as in urban areas. Ninety-seven per cent of the jobs held by the respondents in 1981 and 98 per cent of those held by the time of the interviews in 1982 were in Kassala province, with most of the remaining jobs in the Gezira. Only about 5 per cent of all the jobs reported involved non-farm employment and of these more than a third were herding.

This was true with R.

Table 2.19: Percentage distribution of labourers by place of birth and current home

Place	Place of birth	Current home
Eastern region	11	21
Central region	7	9
Southern region	10	10
Western region[1]	52	49
Ethiopia	19	11
Chad	1	–
Totals	100	100

[1] Northern Darfur (26 per cent), Southern Darfur (30 per cent), Northern Kordofan (32 per cent) and Southern Kordofan (12 per cent).

Table 2.20: Household position of labourers by age group (per cent)

Age group	Head	Son	Brother	Other	Totals
< 20	4	17	2	2	25
20-29	24	21	5	2	52
30-39	14	2	1	0	17
40+	4	0	1	1	6
Totals	46	40	9	5	100

Relationship to household head spans the Head, Son, Brother, Other columns.

Reasons for seeking labouring jobs: the push factors

Table 2.21 confirms that a major factor in forcing people into accepting casual agricultural labouring jobs is the small size of landholdings. While nearly half the sample (which included all but 6 of the refugees interviewed) did not cultivate any personal or family crops in 1982, only 11 per cent farmed more than 20 feddans. Households with large populations did not have significantly greater landholdings.

Table 2.22 demonstrates the priority given to staple food crops. Only 55 per cent of the farmers (28 per cent of the total sample) grew cash crops, and unless the respondent was also the household head he would not control this income. That insufficient or no income from cash-cropping is a major incentive to labour migration was also recognised by ILO/UNDP (1976) which quoted an unpublished survey indicating the total absence of labour migration from two Western Darfur villages which had ample water supplies for extensive year-round vegetable and fruit production for the market. In contrast, about 20 per cent of the male population migrated for at least a month a year from two other Darfur villages with inadequate water supplies which limited the area under cash crops.[12]

Table 2.21: Land areas cultivated in 1982 by respondents
            and their households

Feddans	Per cent of respondents
0	49
1- 4	12
5- 9	13
10-19	15
20-39	7
40+	4
Total	100

The respondents' own reported reasons for engaging in agricultural labouring work not surprisingly emphasise the overriding need for cash (table 2.23). It is interesting that a third of the respondents intended to buy livestock, presumably to increase their income at home and thereby obviate the need to migrate. Thirty-nine men (27 per cent of the unmarried respondents) mentioned earning money for their marriage payments. The lack of references to droughts and crop failure as reasons for doing wage labouring work suggests there are long-term structural reasons producing a large mobile agricultural labour force of young men although this does not preclude the possibility that in years of natural disasters this labour force is dramatically increased.

Male migration from the West and South, in particular, for seasonal agricultural work is made possible by the prevailing system of family farming and the important role women play in agriculture. Table 2.24 shows that while most of the household heads were present for land preparation and planting (tasks in which men are traditionally involved), the weeding and particularly the harvesting and threshing were largely carried out by other family members, the majority of whom would be women. *diff. from irrig.*

Table 2.22: Household or personal crops cultivated
by respondents in 1982

Crops	Per cent of total area cultivated
Dura	50
Millet	13
Groundnuts	18
Sesame	15
Cotton	1
Gum Arabic	2
Vegetables	1
Total	100

Table 2.23: Reported reasons for accepting labouring work

Reasons	Responses	
	Number	Per cent
Money in general	244	43
Personal expenses	120	21
Marriage	39	7
Buy: land	10	2
livestock	90	16
shop	16	3
Build house	2	1
Insufficient land for needs	3	1
Household member ill/died so cash shortage	13	2
Travel/independence/try luck	19	3
Other	9	1
Total	565	100

Little is known of the relative costs and advantages of male migration to their families. Does it increase women's workloads to intolerable levels and what are the costs for women's health, their other work, child-care, their ability to free their children from farm and domestic work to enable them to attend school? Are there non-agricultural male tasks such as house repairs which are neglected, have to be paid for or which also fall to the women?

In the case of the labourers living and farming in the Eastern region the costs of doing labouring work might not be so high. Simpson and Simpson[13] found that the small local cultivators tend to plant and weed earlier than the commercial farmers so as to be available for wage labouring at the period of peak labour demand on the large farms. Some labourers, faced with urgent cash needs, may calculate that it is cheaper to neglect their own weeding (with a consequent drop in yield) rather than pay sheil rates to borrow money (assuming that they are considered credit-worthy enough to obtain a sheil loan. Other small farmers may prefer to reduce their own weeding input (particularly if they have poor land) if the marginal value product of labour in weeding is lower than the on-going wage labouring rate.

The recruitment process

The majority of the large commercial farmers have offices in Gedaref and it is to these that most would-be labourers make their way. About 90 per cent of work agreements are negotiated directly between the employers and labourers. The contractors' role in recruiting labourers from the West and South of the Sudan is reported to have declined in recent years since the refugee influx considerably increased the supply of labour available in the Eastern region. Respondents were recruited by contractors (who were paid 25 piastres per labourer recruited) for only about 5 per cent of jobs. Only one person was given a modest wage advance.

While 12 per cent of the respondents live locally, virtually all of the others travelled to Gedaref with friends or relatives. Group

group.

companionship provides obvious psychological security by sharing the difficulties of looking for work and lodging, withstanding the strains of periods of unemployment, and caring for those who fall sick. However, it is also convenient for the employers since the whole labouring system is built on group hiring and group pressure to produce good work.

Early every morning the labourers gather on the pavements outside the employers' offices, sitting in small groups with their few possesions to hand in case they get work (in any case many of them sleep out in the souk or railway station and therefore keep their personal things with them all the time). A farmer needing labourers will bring a lorry or tractor and trailer to the office and several groups of men will scramble to get in. They are taken to the fields where the wage bargain is negotiated.

There are no fixed daily or piece rates: the payment for each task is negotiated separately for the group as a whole. This consists of a cash and a kind component. The latter includes free lodging in a camp on the farm and staple food supplies (dura flour, oil, salt, onions, chillie, dried fish, dried okra and drinking water) which the labourers cook. The food varies in quality and was worth roughly £S0.50 - 1.00 per person per day in 1982. The cash payments vary for different crops and operations; the average 1981 and 1982 rates were given in the previous section.

The labourers usually first walk round the area to be weeded or harvested before the negotiations start. When bargaining for a weeding task (payment being based on the area covered) they would take into account such factors as the area to be weeded, the weed growth and the extent to which plants are choked, the probability of rain storms since the soil is generally too soft to work the day after the rains and the rainfall would also intensify the weed growth. At harvest, when they are paid by the number of ardebs cut (1 ardeb = 2 ninety kilo bags), they have to consider the plant densities and approximate yields. If the crop is poor it takes longer to harvest as they have to walk further; in such cases the rate per <u>ardeb</u> in 1981 was about £S4.00 compared with £S3.00 for a good crop. They cut and tie bundles of grain which are piled up on a small platform. <u>Their</u> payment is then assessed after the <u>grain has been threshed and bagged</u>.

Various forms of pressure are put on the labourers to settle somewhere near the employers' wage offer. Apart from their own assessment of the supply of unemployed labour in Gedaref, the employer may <u>negotiate with seveal groups at the fields at the same ti</u>me. If || they do not reach an agreement the labourers are expected to walk back || to Gedaref which may be many miles away. Given that they are generally undernourished and they are fed by the employers if they stay and work (and occasionally before the bargaining starts) there is a strong incentive to avoid a long walk in the hot sun. However, after completing the work they collect a note from the agent saying they have done the agreed task and they then have to walk back to Gedaref (or hitch a lift once they reach the main road, if they are lucky) to get their payment from the farmer.

Reported problems of employment on large farms

Most of the problems reported by respondents concerned the cash or kind payment. Two problems require some explanation. After completing a task the labourers return to the farmer's office in Gedaref for payment, carrying a note from the agent to confirm that they have done the work satisfactorily. However, on arrival they ① sometimes find that the farmer is absent or makes excuses to delay payment. This generally causes considerable hardship as the labourers are usually short of money and may well have difficulty in buying food. Moreover, it is impossible for them to accept new work which would take them far from Gedaref again before securing their payment.

The second complaint refers to situations in which farmers are ② reluctant to accept the agent's note at face value and insist on visiting the fields with the labourers to check the work themselves. If they were not satisfied with the work or if, as often happens, it

Table 2.24: Participation in agricultural labour on the family farm

| | Per cent involvement in cultural operations | | |
Operations	1st crop	2nd crop	3rd crop
Land preparation and planting: manual	84	94	100
tractor	8	4	-
Weeding	77	72	75
Harvesting	43	31	32
Threshing	35	28	25
Total number of farmers	135	71	28

has rained heavily again after the labourers had finished and the weeds have regerminated, they would generally insist on the labourers reweeding all or part of the land for no extra payment.

The Labour Officer in Gedaref receives four to six such complaints a day, mainly about employers' alleged defaults in settling the cash component of the agreement or demanding extra work without an additional payment. However, since the Labour Laws specifically exclude agricultural labourers, he advises them that their only redress is to take the case to court. Given the cost of legal fees, the time it would take to get a hearing and the difficulties illiterate labourers (particularly if they are not Arabic speakers) would face in dealing with an unfamiliar court, it is hardly surprising that few take up this option.

Nonetheless, 24 cases claiming a total of £S10,447 were brought before the Gedaref Court between June - October 1982. Of these, 11 cases concerned groups of labourers from the South, 11 from the West and the remaining two were brought by refugees. In one case the plaintiffs claimed to have been paid less than the agreed sum while in the other cases they claimed not to have been paid at all. By the end of October only 7 cases had been resolved. In one case the full amount claimed was paid by the employer while in the others a "compromise" was reached whereby the labourers accepted a lower payment. One farmer was summoned in three of the cases and his brother in another. In three other cases the labourers had only been able to cite the farmers' first names which would presumably make it difficult for the Court to locate and summon them.

It appears that labourers are very vulnerable to exploitation by farmers but in the absence of detailed records of complaints made to the Labour Office it is impossible to estimate the prevalence of these complaints and whether a large number or merely a few mechanised farmers are involved.

V.   Conclusions and recommendations

The operation of the rural labour market for rainfed agriculture in the Eastern region is largely determined by the complementary needs of two inter-dependent farming systems: traditional small-holder production and large-scale mechanised farming schemes. The weeding, harvesting and, to a lesser extent, the threshing on these schemes is carried out by large armies of seasonal labourers who are recruited primarily from a traditional agricultural sector that is unable to meet the subsistence needs of farming households, and secondarily from among the landless Sudanese and refugee populations.

The inter-dependence is both created and reinforced by existing patterns of public and private investment and government intervention, or the lack of it, in the financial, commodity and labour markets. In terms of patterns of investment, there are both regional and sectoral imbalances which have simultaneously created the demand for and supply of agricultural wage labour. These have been exacerbated by the provision of bank credit to commercial farmers at low nominal interest rates which imply zero or even negative real interest rates in the current inflationary situation. This makes the acquisition and operation of machinery cheaper than its real cost. Increased mechanisation of land preparation and seeding permits the expansion of the total area under cultivation, thus increasing the demand for labour for weeding and harvesting. However, as inflation pressures increase the wage bill, cheap credit will eventually result in labour displacing technology.

While cheap credit represents a direct subsidy to the commercial farmers, the lack of a dura marketing and pricing policy can be considered as an important indirect subsidy. The profits realised from speculation, especially for farmers vertically integrated into trading, compensate for the low returns per unit area and make the expansion of mechanised agriculture into marginal land economically feasible. This can only be at the expense of the nomadic herders which raises fundamental questions about social costs and benefits.

At the time of our study there seemed to be a surplus of agricultural wage labourers. The labour shortages reported in earlier years have been largely absorbed by the growing reservoir of refugee labour. The exclusion of agricultural labourers from all labour legislation, including the official minimum wage rates, leaves the labourers vulnerable to possible exploitation by employers.

The implications of all these factors for the Sudanese agricultural sector are disquieting. The increasingly privileged position of the mechanised farming sub-sector has reinforced existing inequalities between large-scale commercial farmers and small, largely subsistence, producers. While there is a growing shortage of fertile arable land in settled areas, the smallholders have neither the capital resources nor the labour necessary to expand into the more distant uncultivated land. Meanwhile commercial farmers, many of whom cultivate between 10,000 and 35,000 feddans, are avoiding state control over land by clearing and cultivating undemarcated land on their own initiative. There are many reported cases of nomadic herders being deprived of pastures and finding their transhumance routes and water points blocked.

The large farmers generally do not practise crop rotations and fallows, with the result that land fertility is not maintained and weed growth becomes a serious problem. In some areas it is no longer economic to cultivate particular weed-infested fields. The result is "land mining" for a number of years before the land is abandoned. However, the original pastures and forests do not regenerate satisfactorily for many years with a consequent substantial loss of land resources and incomes for the nomads and a serious loss to the national economy of both livestock and forestry production.

The very low returns per _feddan_ have two serious implications for the different categories of farmers and for the Sudanese economy as a whole. First, small-holders have no possibility of ever accumulating the savings from agriculture necessary to get out of the cycle of poverty by expanding their farm enterprises with investments in land, machinery, hired labour, chemical inputs and storage facilities. The commercial producers have all drawn their initial capital from non-farming sources such as _sheil_, trading and livestock and their financial success in farming is closely related to their vertical integration into these other economic activities. Second, the poor, unable to provide even adequate subsistence needs from farming, are forced to take on additional occupations both during and after the end of the cultivation season. Since 80 per cent of the rural population is engaged in smallholder production, the market for non-farm goods and services is correspondingly very restricted, which in turn acts as a major constraint on the dynamic expansion of opportunities in the rural labour market.

The position of women in the rural labour market in Eastern Sudan is a matter of some concern given the gross underestimation of their economic role - particularly that of the poorer groups - in the official statistics. This not only involves an undervaluation of the economic importance of some of their domestic work such as threshing, fetching fuel and water, and making mats and baskets but also underestimates their involvement in agriculture as unpaid family workers and their role in petty trading and craft work. Only when their contribution to rural labour processes is fully recognised will it be possible to formulate policies to introduce labour-saving technologies and to promote their access to income-generating activities.

Eastern Sudan has been designated the "bread-basket" of the Middle East, which has justified the allocation of the major share of public and private investment to a commercial farming sector controlled by a small number of farmers who are responsible for the principal share of Sudan's sorghum exports. The benefits in terms of earned foreign exchange, however, seem to be considerably outweighed by the negative impact of this skewed distribution of investment on the traditional farming sector which accounts for 80 per cent of the rural population. The majority of these people live in conditions of extreme poverty from which there is little hope of escape. While grain is being exported by the commercial sector many of the poor are unable to purchase enough of the staple to satisfy subsistence needs. The overriding priority for Sudan's development seems therefore to be new and massive investment in promoting traditional agriculture and linking this to a comprehensive food strategy for the country which would consider integrated policies for staple grain production, home consumption and exports.

Recommendations

Since the interdependence between the two farming systems means that changes in one system will have important consequences for the other, integrated development policies and programmes are called for. The following recommendations cover three areas: labour legislation; monitoring the operation of the rural labour market; and, finally, research to identify and to fill information gaps.

1.   Labour legislation

Section IV drew attention to the major abuses reported by agricultural labourers, the most important of which resulted from the conditions determining the wage bargain. The issues are highly complex and the options for change severely limited by economic and political constraints as the following discussion of possible legislation and its subsequent implementation shows.

Agricultural labourers are at present explicitly exempted from the Sudanese Labour Laws, primarily because of the difficulties of enforcement posed by a largely migrant, unorganised, seasonal labour force working for a few days at a time on limited tasks and scattered in different areas of the Sudan over more than 4 million _feddans_ of mechanised farming schemes and nearly 3 million _feddans_ of irrigated land. However, despite these obvious difficulties of enforcement it seems imperative on grounds of equity that the laws should be extended to include this category of agricultural worker in order to recognise, at least, their rights to legal protection. The major problem then becomes one of implementing these laws, various aspects of which are now examined below.

The first priority would be to set up a system of labour inspection. This could be done in two ways. First, the existing Labour Officers could be given formalised instructions, and if necessary training, in the systematic recording of complaints by agricultural labourers and any subsequent court proceedings. They could be empowered to give advice to the labourers and warnings and advice to employers. Given the high legal costs facing labourers who wish to take court proceedings, it might be advisable for the Labour Officers to have a fund for legal aid to be used in cases where certain employers have had numerous complaints which appear to be well substantiated. Secondly (and preferably), the Sudan could ratify the International Labour Conference Convention 129 concerning Labour Inspection in Agriculture. This would involve setting up a more formal labour inspection system, the functions of which are outlined in Article 6:

"1.   The functions of the system of labour inspection in
        agriculture shall be -

(a)   to secure the enforcement of the legal provisions
      relating to conditions of work and the protection of
      workers while engaged in their work, such as
      provisions relating to hours, wages, weekly rest and
      holidays, safety, health and welfare, the employment
      of women, children and young persons, and other
      connected matters, in so far as such provisions are
      enforceable by labour inspectors;

(b)   to supply technical information and advice to
      employers and workers concerning the most effective
      means of complying with the legal provisions;

(c)   to bring to the notice of the competent authority
      defects or abuses not specifically covered by
      existing legal provisions and to submit to it
      proposals on the improvement of laws and regulations.

2.   National laws or regulations may give labour inspectors in
      agriculture advisory or enforcement functions regarding
      legal provisions relating to conditions of life of workers
      and their families."

The implementation of this system would require the establishment of
guidelines, regulations and in some cases legislation; specialised
training for the labour inspectors in law and aspects of agriculture;
co-ordination with supporting services and government departments such
as the Department of Agriculture; inspection of workers' lodgings,
food, pay and conditions of work.

Generally such a labour inspection system would work closely with
organisations representing employers and workers. While in 1957 the
Sudan ratified the International Labour Conference Convention 98
concerning the Application of the Principles of the Right to Organise
and Bargain Collectively, in practice the only union concerned
directly with persons engaged in agricultural production is the

Farmers' Union which represents the large commercial employers. The difficulties involved in organising an agricultural workers' union are clearly considerable given the ethnic diversity among the refugee and Sudanese migrant labouring population, the generally low educational and literacy levels, and lack of experience with the administrative and legal systems. These handicaps are compounded by the temporary nature of the work, continual movement from farm to farm, the enormous distances between the mechanised and irrigated schemes in the different regions of the country and the high transaction cost of membership for the agricultural workers in these circumstances. Moreover, the distribution of political power could well prove to be a major constraint in establishing such a union.

Despite these difficulties, the enormous size of the migrant agricultural wage labour force, estimated at roughly 800,000 persons a year (ILO/UNIDO, 1976: 90-91) in addition to about 16 per cent of all refugees in the Eastern region (Skills Survey, 1983: Appendix tables A1 - A12) makes it imperative that this category of worker should have a union representing and protecting its interests. Failure to ensure this can only leave them open to potential exploitation and abuses. Since it is clearly difficult for such an organisation to be developed from within the ranks of these workers themselves, it seems essential that the National Federation of Trade Unions should play a major role in establishing and advising such a union. It could be possible for the National Federation to set up a core secretariat which would then establish sub-offices in the main centres of agricultural labouring work such as Gedaref. Most agricultural workers would have to become temporary members although the financing of the whole organisation might well require a direct subsidy from government. While this might be difficult to provide in the current economic recession, the question of equity provides substantial grounds for attempting such a subsidy.

The question of establishing minimum wage rates in line with those for non-agricultural workers is highly complex given the task and piece rate system prevailing in the agricultural sector. While clearly the workers themselves would prefer a fixed daily wage rate which could be legally enforced, it is unlikely that in a situation of labour surplus the employers would wish to substitute daily wage payments for the current system of organising work and remuneration. The former would require more extensive supervision and therefore increased costs.

2.   Monitoring the operation of the rural labour market

At present no comprehensive system exists in the Sudan to monitor the interactions between, and operations of, the urban, rural and foreign labour markets with the result that some sections of the workforce are not covered by labour legislation, and policies devised for one sector of the labour market may well be inconsistent with desirable policies for other sectors.

The main areas that require systematic investigation and the creation of time-series data where possible include:

(a)   The determinants of and linkages between migration to rural, urban and foreign labour markets. It may be necessary to differentiate between different geographical areas and ethnic groups, for example, the poorer agricultural areas of the South and West; the commercial agricultural areas of the Eastern and Central regions; refugees.

(b)   The relationship between the educational system and the supply of and demand for different categories of labour, taking into account remuneration levels, conditions of work and promotion prospects.

(c)   The determinants of relative wages in different sectors and occupations, the role of government policies and legislation.

(d)   The supply of and demand for labour in the agricultural
      sector which is affected by public and private investment
      in development projects; pricing, marketing and taxation
      policies; land tenure and distribution; land rents; export
      policies; mechanisation including the import policies for
      fuel, machinery and spare parts; seasonality factors;
      credit, competition for resources between the crop
      production sub-sector and nomadic livestock production.

(e)   Industrial policies and their effect on labour employment
      and migration.

(f)   Trends in the international demand for Sudanese labour; the
      effect of remittances on the Sudanese economy; implications
      for the supply of and demand for different occupational
      categories in the Sudan.

The size and sophistication with which such a system could be set
up will clearly depend on available finance. If forced to rely on its
own resources, the Sudanese Labour Department could organise the
systematic collection and analysis of such data as already exists
(published and unpublished) in various Ministries, research institutes
and universities. Close co-operation between these institutions could
result in new items of information being elicited from existing
periodic surveys such as the Agricultural Census or the Department of
Agriculture's annual surveys of crop production. Universities and
research institutes could develop co-ordinated research programmes
that complement or fill out gaps in information.

Ideally,   externally-financed technical assistance could be
called on to set up the overall system and possibly to carry out some
in-depth studies of some of the issues listed above since these are
likely to be very costly. In such cases the technical assistance
programme should work in very close conjunction with Sudanese
institutions, affording some additional training functions.

3. <u>Research to identify and fill information gaps</u>

The main areas for future research which emerged from this study include:

(a) A priority need to develop new cultivation, marketing, pricing and credit packages to raise productivity and therefore incomes in the traditional agricultural sector.

(b) To investigate the role of further mechanisation and the use of herbicides in large-scale agriculture, taking into account foreign exchange constraints and the effect on the supply of and demand for agricultural wage labourers in line with Sudan's commitment to promoting full employment.

(c) To examine the pastoral economy and the competition for land, water and forest resources between the nomadic population and the commercial farmers.

(d) To examine the economic and social structures of the main areas of out-migration in the South and West, in order to formulate an integrated policy for the development of these regions as well as the demand for migrant labour in mechanised and irrigated agriculture.

(e) To monitor the role and conditions of work of the refugee population in the rural labour market in the Eastern region.

Footnotes

[1] Nigam (1977) p. 143.

[2] See Simpson and Simpson (1978) pp. 8-9.

[3] See ILO/UNDP (1976) p. 70.

[4] ILO/UNDP (1976) pp. 89-90.

[5] See table 2.10 and Affan (1978) p. 18.

[6] Government of Sudan, Six Year Plan (1977) Vol. 1, p. 23.

[7] ILO/UNDP (1976) pp. 90-91.

[8] Government of Sudan, Six year Plan (1977) Vol. 1, p. 31.

[9] Ibid., Vol. 2, p. 23.

[10] Affan (1978) pp. 4-5.

[11] Ibid., p. 26.

[12] ILO/UNDP (1976) p. 276.

[13] Simpson and Simpson (1978) p. 80.

Appendix to Chapter 2: Tables

Table A 1: Adult equivalent units based on calorie requirements by age and sex

Age group	Sex		
	Male		Female
0 - 2		0.40	
3 - 4		0.48	
5 - 6		0.56	
7 - 8		0.64	
9 - 10		0.76	
11 - 12	0.80		0.88
13 - 14	1.00		1.00
15 - 18	1.20		1.00
19 - 59	1.00		0.88
60+	0.88		0.72

Table A 2: Number and type of occupations by income
category and by gender

Occupation	Rich		Medium		Poor		Total	
	M	F	M	F	M	F	M	F
Farmer	23	3	246	49	162	64	431	116
Farm labourer	-	-	21	-	33	6	54	6
Herder	3	-	16	-	2	-	21	-
Domestic	-	56	2	271	3	201	5	528
Medical	2	1	4	1	1	-	7	2
Teacher	-	-	6	-	1	-	7	-
Driver	16	-	21	-	8	-	45	-
Trader	8	-	52	-	13	-	73	-
Café owner	4	-	9	-	1	-	14	-
Salesman	4	-	20	-	11	-	35	-
Non-farm labourer	-	-	30	-	12	-	42	-
Craftsman	-	-	3	-	2	1	5	1
Tailor	-	-	7	2	7	1	14	3
Hut builder	-	-	12	-	23	-	35	-
Brewer	-	-	-	5	-	7	-	12
Mat/basket maker	-	-	-	8	1	5	1	13
Student	12	4	39	8	19	2	70	14
Disabled/old	2	1	12	6	11	7	25	14
Other	5	-	20	2	15	7	40	9
Total No. of occupations	79	65	520	352	325	301	924	718
Total No. of adults aged 15 and above	59	60	317	288	192	216	568	564

Table A 3: Percentage distribution of occupations by
            income category and by gender

Occupation	Rich		Medium		Poor	
	Male	Female	Male	Female	Male	Female
Farmer	29	4	47	14	50	21
Farm labourer	-	-	4	-	10	2
Herder	4	-	3	-	0.7	-
Domestic	-	86	0.4	76	1	67
Medical	3	2	1	1	0.4	-
Teacher	-	-	1	-	0.4	-
Driver	20	-	4	-	2	-
Trader	10	-	10	-	4	-
Café owner	5	-	2	-	0.4	-
Salesman	5	-	4	-	3	-
Non-farm labourer	-	-	6	-	4	-
Craftsman	-	-	0.6	-	0.7	0.5
Tailor	-	-	1	1	2	0.5
Hut builder	-	-	2	-	7	-
Brewer	-	-	-	1	-	2
Mat/basket maker	-	-	-	2	0.4	2
Student	15	6	8	2	6	1
Disabled/old	3	2	2	2	3	2
Other	6	-	4	1	5	2
Total	100	100	100	100	100	100

Table A 4: Average annual incomes of selected occupations 1981

Occupation	Annual incomes (£S)		
	Average	Minimum	Maximun
Farm labourer	282	25	1,315
Herder	827	150	2,112
Teacher	1,018	600	1,464
Driver	662	50	2,710
Trader	1,206	100	6,100
Restaurant owner	3,871	480	10,800
Tailor	635	60	1,550
Hut builder	345	30	800
Brewer	998	81	3,600
Non-farm labourer	754	90	2,400
Craftsman	462	8	4,800

Table A 5: Distribution of income per capita

£S (Per year)	No.	Per Cent
< 50	4	1.4
50 - 99	39	13.2
100 - 149	41	13.9
150 - 199	44	14.9
200 - 249	37	12.5
250 - 299	25	8.4
300 - 349	22	7.4
350 - 399	20	6.8
400 - 449	13	4.4
450 - 499	9	3.0
500 - 599	6	2.0
600 - 699	6	2.0
700 - 799	6	2.0
800+	24	8.1

CHAPTER 3

The Labour Market in the Gezira Scheme:
A Case Study of Labour Markets in the Irrigated
Agricultural Areas of Sudan

I.   Introduction

The irrigated agricultural schemes in Sudan play a significant
role in determining the level of output and employment in the economy
as a whole.   Not only do they produce the country's major export
crop, cotton; they also account for a substantial proportion of the
rural labour force, especially seasonal migrant labour.   The
large-scale schemes, which are all publicly owned and together cover
more than 3.5 million feddans, are located mainly in the central and
eastern regions of the country, around the banks of the Nile and its
tributaries.   The most important scheme is that of the Gezira with
its Managil Extension, both because of its size (2.1 million feddans)
and because virtually all of the other schemes took the Gezira
production structure as the model.   This chapter is based on a survey
carried out in the Gezira and Managil Extension in September 1982,[1]
and takes the Gezira Scheme as being indicative of the irrigated areas
as a whole.

Although random sampling methods were employed within the
villages selected for survey, the villagers themselves were not
selected through any probability based sampling procedure.   Three
villages were selected which had many tenants in their population.
Three others were selected because they were labour camps, the
population being composed of Fellata and Burgo.   Within the villages,
the village elders were consulted as to the approximate distribution
of rich, medium and poor inhabitants.   A sample was then made from a
village list, using a random number system.   Attempts were made to

ensure that the proportions of rich, medium and poor households were the same as reported for the whole population.   In the case of the ethnically mixed Fellata villages, we also tried to represent the ethnic differentiation in the sample.   Table 3.1 shows the nature of the sample, which covered 162 households.

Table 3.1

Village	Number of people in the sample	Percentage of sample households to total village households	Percentage of sample
Nueila	410	25	31.56
Cambo Daoud	90	5	6.93
Wakara	329	11	25.33
Remeitab	267	10	20.55
Remeitab Fellata	39	10	3.00
Kimeir Adam	164	25	12.62
Total	1 299	-	100.00

Nueila, Wakara and Remeitab are villages where many of the people are tenants; Cambo Daoud and Kimeir Adam are labour camps established in their own right; while Remeitab Fellata, as the name suggests, is a fellata section of Remeitab village.   Nueila is on the road from Hassaheisa to Managil, about 30 km from Managil but on the edge of the Gezira Main Scheme.   Cambo Daoud is in Managil Extension, about 15 km west of Managil.   Wakara is roughly 15 km south of El Dueim. Remitab and Remeitab Fellata are about 35 km south east of Barakat, while Kimeir Adam is near to them.

The general characteristics of the sample indicate that the Gezira population is a very young one (more than 60 per cent below the age of 20 years and another 23 per cent between the ages of 20 and 40

years) with a high dependency ratio.   It is also remarkably literate,
with about 53 per cent of the inhabitants able to read and write to a
functional level.[2]

II.   The irrigated areas: history and relation
      to other forms of production in the Sudan

Sudan became a major grower and exporter of cotton for a number
of reasons.   These reasons are not entirely separable, and none is
entirely paramount.   Following reconquest by the British in 1899,
Sudan   posed   considerable   problems   for   the   Anglo-Egyptian
administration.   Major issues included (1) the need to hold on to
Sudan militarily in order to safeguard British control of Egypt and of
the Red Sea route to India; (2) the need to ensure that the
administration and defence of this vital link in the Imperial chain
did not place an undue burden on the metropolitan economy, but was, as
far as possible, self-financing; and (3) the necessity to maintain
internal order and control, as a condition for the pursuit of the
first two aims - this in the aftermath of what had been a major war,
involving a defeat of British-supported Turco-Egyptian forces in
1885.   Although it would be facile to describe the Mahdist State and
the Mahdist movement as having been simply a proto-nationalist
movement, it certainly had unified and organised large elements of the
diverse Sudanese population in opposition to foreign rulers.   In
these circumstances, it was not possible for the Anglo-Egyptian
administration to ensure control over a long period by military means
alone.   It was necessary to use the existing divisions within
Sudanese society to tie the economic interest of sympathetic groups to
the new, foreign administration.   It is in this situation that the
development of irrigated agriculture in the Gezira had one of its
firmest roots.

The second major root which gave rise to the massive development
of irrigated agriculture was the need to defend the declining British
textile industry.   This industry which had played the role of
leading sector in the accumulation of industrial capital in Britain,

was by the late nineteenth and early twentieth century showing signs
of decline and uncompetitiveness, as methods and machinery became
outmoded and latecomers to the industry in other countries became more
competitive in an expanding world market.   Thus, the most explicit
rationale for the development of the Gezira area can be detected in
the debates in the British Parliament, where Lancashire MPs expressed
the need for policies which would benefit Lancashire - "Lancashire"
meaning (a) the existing textile manufacturers; (b) the manufacturers
of textile spinning and weaving machinery; (c) the workers in those
industries who were facing unemployment.   The outcome was a shift in
policy aimed at moving into the finer end of the market, in which
Lancashire still retained some degree of comparative advantage and
ensuring the supply of fine cotton (long and extra long staple) in the
face of declining Egyptian production and competition from non-British
manufactures in the international market place.   These multiple
influences led to the establishment of the vast irrigation
infrastructure in central Sudan.   An additional factor which
contributed to the final form of production, and thus of relations of
production, was the strongly paternalistic attitude of the Sudan
Political Service which ensured that external, non-Sudanese
speculators should not be allowed to gain control of land in the
newly, or soon to be, irrigated areas.

The precise form of production relationship established in the
Gezira can be described in various ways.   Gaitskell described it in
official terms as a "partnership".   In the colonial period, the
partnership was said to be one between Government, private enterprise
(in the form of the two concessions companies - the Sudan Plantations
Syndicate and the Kassala Cotton Comapny) and the Sudanese
cultivators, known collectively as "the tenants".   It should be
pointed out that the partnership was not an equal one, with tenants
having to accept the terms laid down by the Gezira Board.   This
system continued until June 1980, when the Government announced the
abolition of the joint account system with effect from the 1981/82
season, and its replacement by an individual account system whereby
tenants are charged for each input for each crop.

The labour market in the irrigated areas is only to some degree a "local" market. The degree to which it is local in the sense of reflecting purely local elements of supply, demand and resource endowment may be very small indeed. At its peak of geographical influence the Gezira Scheme drew labour from 3,000 miles across the Sahelian belt into Northern Nigeria, Chad and Senegal. Such a wide geographical spread is by and large no longer the case, although the result of such wide-ranging sources of labour is still very evident in the presence of settled "migrant" labour villages or camps, the people of which are referred to collectively as "Fellata" and "Burgo". In the other direction, and much more recently, the labour market in the irrigated areas is now affected by the rapid urbanisation in the Sudan, together with the increased demand during the past ten years for certain categories of labour from other Middle Eastern countries, notably the Gulf and Libya (see Appendix I).

In terms of the framework outline in Chapter 1, the irrigated areas can be seen as one of the nodal transaction points within a system of interlocking forms of production, each one producing labour and other commodities under certain specific conditions, and having some of that labour selectively removed. The relations between these forms of production (with their characteristic labour markets) were schematised in Chapter 1. From that discussion it was evident that, geographically, the chain of labour supply runs predominantly from the west to the east and from the south to the north. However, migrants from Darfur, Kordofan and the southern provinces are not the only seasonal labourers attracted to the irrigated areas. Peasants from traditional agriculture in the central and eastern areas, as well as nomadic groups, may be forced to supplement their income from traditional occupations to ensure economic survival.

III. The demand for labour

The contract between the individual tenant and the Sudan Gezira Board is central to the pattern of cultivation as well as the operation of the labour market. Tenancy is allocated on an

individual basis, automatically renewable on satisfactory performance
in the preceding season.   Usually this criterion refers to cotton
cultivation.   The rate of annual evictions has always been very low,
rarely more than one per cent.   It has always been expected that the
tenants would provide the main labour input to the tenancy, with
additional help from paid labourers at the two cultivation peaks of
weeding (September–December) and harvesting (January–May).   It is
this expection and obigation which forms the core mechanism of the
labour market in the Gezira.

The required cotton acreage for each tenant is specified by the
SGB.   For some years it has been apparent that from the point of view
of the tenant household, the cultivation of cotton is at best
financially marginal.   It has also been a source of economic
differentiation between tenant households, because in some cases
tenants have experienced continuing losses from cotton cultivation.
This implies that such tenants do only the minimum necessary (in
cotton cultivation) to ensure the annual renewal of their tenancies,
and so safeguard their access in the next season to land devoted to
other crops.   The most important of these other crops include dura,
cultivated for food security, and wheat and groundnuts cultivated as
cash crops.

In all cases, the demand for hired labour from tenant households
is dependent upon a number of factors.   Firstly, there is the
availability of labour within the tenant household.   This depends on
the demographic distribution of the household (stage of the
developmental cycle as well as other factors such as emigration or
illness of members), the willingness of members to work without
additional wages and involvement of members in full-time education or
other activities.   Secondly, there is the question of the seasonality
of agricultural operations, especially the height and width of the
seasonal peaks of labour requirement.   The sharper and thinner such
peaks are, the more are tenant households likely to demand additional
labour in cultivation.

Given the demographic nature of the developmental cycle of households, it is the group of tenant households where the head is below the age of 45 and above the age of 54[3] which is most likely to demand labour at times other than the harvest, when all households require supplementary labour inputs. Insofar as the small sample of the 1982 survey is representative of the age structure of the whole population of Gezira tenants, 66 per cent were in the group of tenant households most likely to demand additional labour. In the coming years, the balance of household to non-household labour may become even less favourable, particularly if tenant cultivation is not an attractive proposition for the younger generation.

Allied to this is the fact that even household labour is not always free for the household head. It has been pointed out that in the Gezira a male child, from about the age of 19 and certainly after marriage, usually receives some payment for work from the household head.[4] In some cases this can even approach or equal the market wage rate. For a female child, the period of contribution as an unpaid farm worker is briefer, up to the age of marriage, which is probably around 16. However, her contribution as an unpaid domestic worker starts early on and continues until she leaves her parental home to join that of her husband.

Thus demographic characteristics as well as the pattern of agricultural seasonality indicate that the average tenant household in the Gezira will require some additional labour for at least part of the year and possibly throughout the year. The actual level of effective demand or labour depends both on the physical labour requirements of cultivation (given a particular cropping pattern) and on the financial ability of tenant households to pay for hired labour.

In table 3.2 some estimate of the required labour input for various crops are recorded. It is interesting to compare these estimates with the results of the ILO 1982 survey, presented in table 3.3 below.

Table 3.2: Labour requirements by crop, Gezira

| Crop | Area | | Labour requirement | | |
	000 feddans	% of total	Total (million man-days)	% of total	Man-days per feddan
Long staple cotton	383.1	29.2	22.4	47.5	58.5
Medium staple cotton	52.3	4.0	2.4	5.1	46.0
Wheat	267.9	20.4	1.7	3.6	6.2
Groundnuts	264.2	20.1	12.1	25.6	45.8
Dura	343.8	26.2	8.6	18.2	25.0
Total	1 311.3	100	47.2	100	—

Sources: Euroconsult (1981, p. 51)
Sudan Gezira Board (1982, pp. 19-30).

Table 3.3: Labour days used in the cultivation of 3 main crops

Crop	Household labour per feddan (x days)	% of total labour	Non-household labour per feddan (x days)	% of total labour	Total labour per feddan (x days)	Crop as % of total labour per feddan
Cotton	21.04	16.99	44.30	35.79	65.34	52.80
Dura	14.00	11.32	16.75	13.53	30.75	24.84
Groundnuts	13.86	11.22	13.82	11.16	27.68	22.36

Source: Survey 1982

The very large difference between the Euroconsult figure for groundnuts and that of the present study, probably reflects the fact that tenants are not entirely aware of the labour inputs to that crop, as so many of them sharecrop. Those figures are, of course, over-all labour inputs. However, only a certain percentage of household labour is in fact non-remunerated. The demand for paid non-household labour is what concerns us here, and it is to an estimate of this that we must now turn. One estimate which has been made, based on SGB economic surveys, is also to be found in the Euroconsult Report 1982. The following table provides an estimate of tenant family labour as a percentage of total labour input during the seasons 1976/77 to 1980/81 inclusive, by crop.

Table 3.4

Season	Cotton	Wheat	Ground-nuts	Dura
76-77	25	48	26	22
77-78	22	52	37	32
78-79	28	55	32	22
79-80	30	45	20	29
80-81	36	52	29	37
Average rounded down	28	50	29	28

Source: Euroconsult (1981), Vol. II, p. 154

Using this as the basis, we can calculate the total labour requirement of the Scheme, based on 1979-80 areas planted, as being 51,151,326 person days per year. Allowing pro rata reductions for each crop in line with the above estimates of proportion of household labour per crop, the total demand for person days of hired labour per years would be in the region of 34,975,673.

Given the technological labour requirements and the structure of
the tenant households, the third important factor affecting labour
demand is the financial position of the tenants. This is affected by
both the liquidity and capital profile of the households, and the
payments system to the Gezira tenants. These three factors together
determine (a) the ability of tentants to demand labour in the market;
(b) the terms on which the labour is demanded – the labour contract;
(c) the ability to operate the tenancy efficiently, given the crucial
motion between, for example, timely weeding and picking of yield of
cotton and other crops.[5]

The payment system in the Gezira Scheme has always been
complex. It consists of five types of payment spread over the
year. The five categories of payment are: profits, appreciation,
cultivation advances, picking advances and advances to help with
pulling out Those payments are not uniform in amount, and not all
tenants receive all of them. For example, a tenant may not in fact
make a profit, for the appreciation payments (based on the actual
price realised for the previous year's crop) may not be very large.
The cultivation advances may not cover the actual costs of
cultivation, notably of weeding, particularly if the specific
conditions on a tenancy demand more labour than has been allowed for
by the SGB estimates. The complexitiy and variability of the
payments means that for many tenants the actual amounts to be expected
are unclear as is their precise purpose. Thus, they are often
regarded as, and used for, day-to-day household expenses.

Overall, this system of payments gives rise to what can be called
"stress periods" in the tenants' annual household budget cycle. Two
main stress periods are identifiable. One is from August to the end
of November, during the growth period of most crops, when timely and
efficient weeding and watering is necesary if yields are not to
suffer. The other is from February to April during the harvest, when
once again, timely and efficient work is necesary to ensure maximum
yields and thus incomes. These stress periods, especially in the
case of those households where little household labour is available,

drive tenants into various kinds of debt, either in the form of simple borrowing or in the form of forward selling. Those stress periods effect the body of tenants in different ways, depending on their underlying resource endowments, their particular cropping strategy and the consequent requirements for credit.

Examination of the capital profile of Gezira tenant households reveals substantial differentiation. S.A. Ahmed (1977) identified seven categories of tenants, based on asset endowment, involvement in major off-farm activities such as large-scale trading, and involvement in vegetable production. These seven groups exhibited widely differing patterns in the amount and seasonality of credit requirement as well as in the amount, timing and source of income. The two groups with the highest asset endowments, who also had income from major off-farm activities, never experienced a capital deficit in the course of a year's production. By contrast, for all of the other groups the capital deficit increased with time from the beginning of the cultivation cycle in June. It reached a maximum in March for those tenants whose off-farm income was either non-existent or consisted of petty trade, and in November for the group of tenants whose initial asset endowment was categorised as "medium" but who had some major involvement in big business.[6] From Ahmed's work it is apparent that off-farm activities are an important source of income for almost all tenant households, and in particular for the poorest group, which often sells its labour to other tenants.

Capital deficits of Gezira tenants have an important effect on the labour market. Thus a substantial proportion of the farm income of poor tenants may be absorbed by their need to borrow money at high interest rates in order to finance the cultivation. The continuation of low overall income and high interest rates in turn implies that these groups will have to supplement their farm income by off-farm activities, in particular by working as labourers on the farms of other tenants.

Tenant farmers with low assets are thus caught in a scissors whereby they are only able to hire in labour on the basis of credit obtained at high cost; they use more family labour than the other groups because they are unable to demand as much hired labour as they might require; at the same time, they are compelled to engage themselves as hired labourers to other farmers in order to finance their subsistence needs and to repay their debts.[7] Most of the credit for such farmers is on the basis of _sheil_ transactions, which involve high real rates of interest.

Having established the underlying factors in the dynamics of the tenant household, we can now turn to a schematic description of the types of production strategy with regard to labour use in which this results.

There are four broad categories of labour available to tenants.[8] These are:

(i) paid labour living outside the village in the labour settlements. This consists of Fellata or Burgo, predominantly non-Arab workers;

(ii) migrant labourers from villages outside the scheme. These people are predominantly Arab and some non-Arab westerners, resident for most of the year in rain-fed agricultural areas;

(iii) labourers resident in the Gezira villages;

(iv) members of the tenants' families.

Based on these four types of labour, four broad input mixes are apparent:

(i) exclusive use of labour from outside the village - Fellata or Burgo for cultivation and irrigation, migrant labourers for the harvest;

   (ii)   use of a few, full-time workers from the villages
          supplemented by migrant labourers for the harvest. In
          both cases, they will probably have had a long-term
          relationship with the employer. In the case of the
          village labourers, there may be a kinship relationship.
          However, this does not seem to have been significant in
          affecting the wage rate, although in some cases it may
          affect the precise form of the contract between employer
          and employee;

   (iii) near exclusive use of household labour, supplemented by
          other labourers during the harvest period;

   (iv)   the use of a large number of people from the village. The
          make-up of this group will vary from day to day, and will
          be assembled on an _ad hoc_ basis depending on the cash flow
          and liquidity of the tenant. Once again, this is likely
          to be supplemented during the harvest period.

Each of these four broad strategies can be divided into sub-types.
Those reflect the different economic and social circumstances of the
individual tenant household, and in particular their specific set of
social and financial resources. These sub-divisions may be described
as follows:

1.1 A wealthy tenant who runs his tenancy on an entrepreneurial
basis, most probably as one enterprise of a number. Such a tenant
may also have, for example, an interest in trading, a mill or a
lorry. Such a tenant will employ labour from outside the village for
most of the year. This labour in all likelihood will be resident in
the labour camps. Some of these labourers will be employed for quite
lengthy periods, in particular for the whole three or four months of
the weeding season, and when irrigation is most necessary, during the
establishment and growth of the crops.

    It is apparent that it is the wealthier tenants who adopt this
strategy. A widely held view is that it is easier to get the maximum
work out of labourers from outside the village. In some cases, the

relationship between employer and employee consists not only of cash payments, but also the provision of housing. Some tenants actually build and maintain houses in the labour camps, and this forms an element of the contract between employer and employee.

It is certainly the case that if entrepreneurial tenants are adopting this strategy, then it is because it is easier to hold these labourers to a certain standard of work. There are no internal village, non-market relationships such as kinship, to enter into the bargain. From the labourers' point of view, this type of employment is attractive. Such an employer is unlikely to have cash flow or liquidity problems and is not entirely dependent on payment from the SGB. Thus payment is unlikely to be delayed at the completion of work. Indeed, advances and loans for subsistence purposes may be available, particularly when the relationship between employer and employee is one of long standing.

1.2 Some tenants will be able to underake a good proportion of the work alone. They will still, however, require help at peak periods such as at harvest and during weeding. They choose to use paid labour for a number of reasons. The main reason is that they do not have sufficient household labour available. They also feel that they get better work from non-village labour, and that the relationship is uncomplicated by intra-village social ties. However, although they wish to use extra-village labour, they face problems of liquidity and cash flow, particularly if the tenancy is their main source of income. Labourers require assurances with regard to payment. The outcome of this type of situation is often a share-cropping contract with the labourers.

There are various forms of sharecropping. In this case, it is frequently the _dura_ crop which is shared, but increasingly, because of its high value, groundnuts are shared. From the tenants' viewpoint, the best strategy to adopt in such circumstances (bearing in mind that there is no other source of income than the tenancy) is to use the labourers to cultivate the _dura_, and pay them with a larger than 50-50 share of the groundnuts. By means of this strategy, the tenant ensures a full return from dura – which assures the basic subsistence crop – while still receiving some return from the groundnuts.

If, however, the tenant has to share-crop both dura and groundnuts, then the situation is very unfavourable, for such tenants will only receive approximately 50 per cent of each crop, and later in the year will be forced to purchase dura for household consumption at the ruling market price.

1.3 A tenant who has little cash or assets, low social standing, and few or no sources of credit, may also be in the position of having to employ non-village labour. This is particularly the case if there is no source of income other than the tenancy. Such tenants differ in the strategy that they adopt from those in category 1.2 above, insofar as they prefer not to enter into crop-sharing arrangements. Because their credit rating is low, they are likely to find some difficulty in employing labourers, particularly labourers from the labour camps. They will be under immediate pressure to pay their workers.

This category of tenants is more likely to enter into a combination of mortgage (sheil) of dura and cotton. They will use this cash for household expenses, while attempting to live off the advances from the SGB. Such tenants are in a very difficult position, and find themselves in debt to the SGB which under the new individual account system is likely to carry over from year to year.

It can be noted from the above that both wealthy, well-connected tenants and quite poor tenants use apparently similar strategies, but for different reasons. For a wealthier tenant, whose tenancy is just one enterprise among several, the employment of extra-village labour is more probably a way of maximising returns. For the poor tenant, dependent on the tenancy as the sole or main source of income, the employment of extra-village labour is the only way to stay in the game, and retain access to the tenancy, to a landholding, by meeting the minimal requirement to cultivate cotton.

2.   The second type of labour strategy is to use a few people from the village on a regular year-to-year basis, with some supplementation, particularly at harvest, from migrant labourers. The key to this strategy is in the extra-economic relationships which such a tenant has with the labourers.   These regularly employed village labourers are likely to be friends, relatives or their children.   Within this category two sub-types may be identified. These are:

2.1 An elderly tenant with some inherited wealth, or widely known to have good credit standing, uses a few people from the village who are tied to him by kinhsip, friendship, or by "quasi-kin" links.   By this latter term is meant a specific relationship, that between one family and another which in the past was slave to the former.   Now, of course, there is no such thing as slavery, it is indeed a thing of the distant past.   However, elements of the old relationship remain in terms of some of the old feelings of recriprocal obligations.

The most important feature which influences this type of tenants' position in the employment of labour is the ability to borrow money to finance operations.   Often such a tenant will be able to borrow from friends or relatives who have salaried posts.   Such tenants are also likely to occupy minor administrative positions, such as on the village council, and thus in certain circumstances to be able to perform favours for others, particularly for those who work for them.

The main point here is that there is by no means a purely market relationship between this type of employer and the labour force. Factors of kinship, friendship and patronage also enter into the transaction.

A variant of this strategy is when a tenant is unable to recruit quite enough labour from the village.   He will therefore combine village labour on a regular basis with some hired labour from outside the village.   He is, however, in a more advantageous position with regard to this extra-village labour than a tenant in category 1.3 because of his known ability to borrow cash, and thus to pay promptly.   This facilitates the making of the contract, and probably avoids the necessity of entering into sharecropping agreements.

2.2   The second sub-category of tenants who predominantly use a small group of villages for the work is those tenants of the ex-slave families.   Unless they are wealthy (and a few are), in which case they will follow strategy 1.1, this group will use the labour of their household plus that of other unrelated ex-slave villagers.   They are restricted in their ability to employ labour within the village in part by a certain reluctance on the part of village labourers to enter their employment.

3.   The third main category of labour strategy is that of the tenants who are able to work their tenancy entirely by means of family labour.   As has been suggested above, these are few in number, and their ability to do this is transient, reflecting the stage of development of their household.   Clearly, their demand for labour will be small, although they will need additional labour during the harvest.

4.   The fourth category of labour strategy consists of those tenants who use a large number of different people from within the village. In reality they have a constantly changing ad hoc labour force.   They employ little labour from outside the village.   Typically, these people are among the poorest, often strangers to the local area, with few social or economic resources with which to enter the market. They will accrue debts to the SGB and will be likely to have to enter share-cropping arrangements in the event of employing any extra-village labour at all.   This strategy may be characteristic of female-headed households.

These then are the constraints on the effective demand for labour, and the resultant labour strategies.   These are the resources with which the labour purchasers enter the market.   These give rise to the observed patterns of labour use in the villages in the Gezira scheme. A total of 40 interviews conducted by Taha El Jack Taha among the farmers in the Gezira in October 1982 and referring to the 1981-82 season, indicated that the following conclusions are valid:

(i)   minor land preparation operations are usually carried out
      by the tenants themselves, together with local village
      labour and labourers from the labour camps;

(ii) the labourers from the labour camps often enter into
      sharecropping arrangements with tenants as part of the
      overall labour contracts;

(iii) the only period when labour seems to be needed from outside
      the Gezira-Managil area is during the cotton picking season.

IV. The supply of labour

As mentioned earlier, there are three broad categories of labour
available in Gezira agriculture besides the labour drawn from tenant
households and exchanged between them.   These three categories are
the labourers within Arab villages in the irrigated areas, labourers
from the labour camps, and seasonal migrant labourers, who are
especially relevant for cotton-picking and related activities.

The Arab villagers

An account of the Arab villagers to today must be placed in the
context of the social structure of the Gezira-Managil area prior to
irrigation.   A brief description is outlined below.[9]   The economic
base of the area consisted of subsistence agriculture, primarily
rainfed dura using terrace methods for the preservation of the sparse
rainfall.   This was combined with some transhumant cattle keeping.
In some areas, the majority of the people would leave their villages
in the dry season in order to search for pasture with their flocks.
This was the general picture, although where people were settled near
the river, an element of irrigated agriculture would have been
present.   This was traditionally done on a share-cropping basis
between the landowner, the labourers and the the owner of the
Shaduf.   Within this production structure, there is evidence of some
not inconsiderable degree of social differentiation.   Land was not
always held on a traditional variable usufruct basis.   In many cases,

a particular man or household would have title to quite considerable areas of rainland.   Probably, most Arabs had rights to some land for their subsistance purposes, but in some cases considerable areas were held by individuals.   The land would have been worked by household labour in the case of small, subsistence households.   In the case of the large landowners, the work would have been done by household labour, plus the household slaves, thus enabling the large areas to be culivated.   It should not be forgotten that the Gezira area was certainly a grain surplus area, providing this surplus for consumption in the towns during the Mahdist period.

So much for the past.   What of its implications for the present?   The initial distribution of tenancies allowed for the very large landowners to receive a maximum of four.   After this allocation had been made, some of the non-landowning members of the community could receive tenancies.   In the ensuring 50 or so years, these distributions have undergone change.   During the bad years of the 1930s many tenancies were abandoned, and various forms of transfer have occurred.   The main point is that by no means all inhabitants received tenancies.   A large group remained whose only source of income was from labouring or from some other trading or artisan activity.   With the exception of a few scattered areas, there was not even access to <u>bildat</u> land as almost all land in the irrigated area was taken into the Scheme.   In the sample of villages surveyed in 1982, only 1.29 of the households had <u>bildat</u> land.   In effect, then, the development of the Gezira Scheme created a class of labourers who no longer had rights to land for their minimal subsistence purposes. In addition, with the break-up of the larger units of land, traditional reciprocal obligations were eroded.   Slowly, the non-tenants have become more and more like free wage labourers, although as was noted in the previous section many non-market elements may still enter into the labour contract between some tenants and some labourers.

The range of household incomes found in the 1982 survey among the labourers in the Arab villages exhibited a distribution from £S227 to £S1,960 per year, with a mean of £S1,193.   This is below the mean

household income of even the smaller tenants - those with less than
five feddans of cotton, whose mean household income was found to be
£S1,829 from all sources. The labourers are less well-off than the
poorest group of tenants.

The labourers from the labour camps

According to the Survey of Labour Camps,[10] the present
population of the labour camps is 169,992, with an average population
of 235 people per camp. This gives an average of 1,603 per block and
12,142 per group. The labour camp population thus comprises about
13.5 per cent of the total population of the irrigated area. 71,056
(41 per cent) are said to be of working age.

These people are predominantly engaged in agriculture or
agriculture-related occupations (87 per cent). 43 per cent of them
are relied upon in certain blocks for cotton picking and the groundnut
harvest, 26.0 per cent in weeding, 21.6 per cent in stevedoring and
18.3 per cent in cotton stalk eradication.

The standard of public health in these camps is very poor.
Housing is cramped, refuse accumulates, and the people use the canals
as their main water source. Other than these bare facts,
surprisingly little is known about the labour camps and their
population in the irrigated areas. They are a constant part of the
scene, but detailed information as to their role in the labour market
is sparse. Some glimpses are available which bear witness to their
central importance to the Scheme over a very long period.[11] These
indicate that there has been historically some degree of competition
and possible antagonism between labourers in such camps and those from
the Arab villages. Compared with the latter, within the labour camps
there was not only a much narrower spread of occupations (mainly
agricultural wage labour) but also considerably less evidence of
secondary and tertiary occupations. So one set of villages
(including some but not all of the Arab villages) could be seen as
notably wealthier overall, with salaried employees among its members;

the rest were poorer, consisting of people mainly dependent upon the sale of their labour.

However, the present study suggests a different tendency. The table below provides evidence that for the villages surveyed in 1982, the average number of occupations per household head increased, the less resources the household head had, or the closer the household head was to being a pure wage labourer.

Table 3.5: Mean, median and modal number of occupations per household head by certain occupational categories

Occupational category	Tenants	Arab labourers	Fellata sharecroppers	Fellata labourers
Mean	1.36	1.72	2	2.07
Median	1	2	2	2
Modal	1	2	2	2

Source: 1982 Survey

This would suggest that the groups have different survival strategies, reflecting their different resource bases and their different income earning capacities, and more importantly, the predictability of that income earning capacity. Indeed, table 3.5 could be read as representing a continuum from the more secure (tenants) to the less secure (Fellata labourers). The Arab labourers are more secure because of their non-market links with employers.

In fact, it is quite likely that the income of the labourers is actually understated. This could be for a number of reasons: such as the general tendency for people to understate their income and the involvement of many labourers in a range of sharecropping arrangements with tenants.

Some twenty years ago it may have been possible to conclude as did Brausch et. al. (1964) that there was not a great difference between those dependent on one tenancy alone and those dependent on

the sale of their labour.   Today there is a difference but it is not
entirely consistent.

In the tables which follow, it should be noted that Wakara
village, situated in the White Nile Corporation area has a standard
holding size of six feddans of cotton, and exhibits consistently lower
income than the two Gezira tenant villages, Nueila and Remeitab.   In
addition, the Wakara values for income are quite similar to the
wealthier Fellata village, Kimeir Adam.

The following table shows the distribution of total household
head income by village.   Cambo Daoud, Remeitab Fellata and Kimeir
Adam are all migrant labour villages; the others are tenant
villages.   It is clear from this table that the mean household head
income is higher in the villages of Nueila, Remeitab and Wakara than
it is in the other three; that the range of incomes is greater in the
first group; and that with the exception of Wakara, the first and
third quartiles are higher in the former group than in the latter.

Table 3.6:   Total income of the household head in the labour camp
              villages (£S p.a.)

Village	Nueila (1)	Remeitab (2)	Wakara	Cambo Daoud	Remeitab Fellata (3)	Kimeir Adam (4)
Maximum	38 225	3 676	5 064	2 184	1 056	6 174
Third quartile	1 960	1 718	1 289	831	1 030	1 447
Mean	2 446	1 296	1 190	677	785	1 225
First quartile	465	576	528	426	411	607
Minimum	15	58	30	197	255	137

Source: 1982 Survey.

(1) This is highly leptokurtic at 32.03: there is one very wealthy
entrepreneur in the village.
(2) Approximates to normal distribution.
(3) Negatively skewed at 1.88.
(4) Leptokurtic at 11.72

Table 3.7 shows similar features for total household incomes by village.

Table 3.7: Total household income by village (£S p.a.)

Village	Nueila	Remeitab	Wakara	Cambo Daoud	Remeitab Fellata	Kimeir Adam
Maximum	38 225	4 622	10 205	2 476	1 079	6 174
Third quartile	2 744	2 919	1 551	1 346	1 073	1 679
Mean	2 932	2 006	1 580	997	835	1 378
First quartile	855	1 110	554	550	429	607
Minimum	120	414	36	204	255	137

Source: 1982 Survey

When we come to look at agricultural income alone, table 3.8, we see a number of features.

Table 3.8: Household head agricultural income by village (£S p.a.)

Village	Nueila	Remeitab (1)	Wakara	Cambo Daoud	Remeitab Fellata	Kimeir Adam
Maximum	5 242	1 848	4 273	750	450	5 350
Third quartile	982	1 427	890	195	401	1 026
Mean	844	839	682	191	219	926
First quartile	95	297	110	95	78	217
Minimum	15	2	5	60	70	60

Source: 1982 Survey

(1)   Negatively skewed

Mean household head agricultural incomes in the two villages of Neuila and Remeitab are markedly higher than in Cambo Daoud and Remeitab Fellata; and mean household head agricultural income in Kimeir Adam exceeds that in all three tenant villages. The situation today then is in all probability not very different from that reported in 1963 as far as the agricultural income of household heads is concerned. But, when total household income is considered, the tenant households are better off than the labour camp households.

We can now consider the nature of contracts by which labourers enter the markets. There are a number of factors which enter into that contract. These are ethnic differentiation, class differentiation, the 'semi-organised' nature of the migrants, and the view of them all as a 'reserve' of labour.

As a population of foreign origin, linguistically and culturally distinct from the people of the Gezira, the migrants are obviously very visible. They are, in addition, like many ethnic minorities in many places, the object of a whole range of stereotypes, myths and misunderstandings of what these very real cultural differences mean. Thus, they are considered variously to be particularly holy and religious, some are considered fekkirs. They are also considered to be a health hazard, to have loose morals and to be unduly involved in the brewing of merissa. Thus, the migrants' cultural differences became identified with negative attitudes attaching to their economic position within the structure of the Scheme.

From the evidence above, it is by no means clear that in terms of income, the migrants occupy a totally different status position from the average labourer in the area. However, their communities appear to be less differentiated in terms of income distribution than are the Arab villages, the range being narrower. But this is not the central feature of their class relationship with the Arab villages. The central feature is that the tenant could be said to have a higher degree of economic security, having something which few migrants possess - a right to land.

Because of the economic constraints of the tenancy, discussed in Section III, many tenants enter into sharecropping agreements with their labourers, both from the village and from the labour camps. This is not a recent development, but it may have increased in incidence in recent years.

Certainly, from the perspective of the labourers, sharecropping provides a means of gaining access to land either for cash or subsistence cropping, without at the same time having to carry the burdens associated with the tenancy agreement. Indeed, in the 1982 survey, almost 100 per cent of the labour camp households were found to have sharecropping arrangements with tenants. Thus, the tenant does not by and large occupy the position simply of employer in relation to the labourer. In many cases, the tenant is in effect indebted to the labourer, and repays the debt by entering into a sharecropping arrangement. Given the overall dependence on labour which characterises the migrants owing to their general absence of tenurial rights, they are bound to drive as favourable a bargain as they can. And the work for which they are most likely to be in demand, weeding, harvesting and pulling out is precisely the work upon which the time constraints are greater, and for which they will be most able to drive a hard bargain. Looked upon by the SGB for many years as a 'reserve' of labour, it is unlikely that, since very early in the Scheme's history, they have been anything but a _vital_ source of labour. In this respect their social position is further complicated, for they compete with local villagers who are also labourers. Thus, it is not surprising that while all three categories, average tenants (mean = £S1,829), village labourers (mean = £S1,193) and labour camp labourers (mean = £S1,115) share very similar household income levels, they are set against each other by the structure of production relations in the Scheme. In effect, there exists a culturally segmented labour force on the one hand (tenants versus migrant labourers) and a status divided but often kinship related and certainly culturally related labour force on the other (tenants versus village labouers). The position of all three groups in the process of production is not, however, essentially dissimilar.

The contracts by which the two kinds of labourers are bound are not markedly different in their distribution. The folllowing table summarises the types of contract typical of both Arab and camp labourers.

Table 3.9: All labourers: per cent type of contract for main occupation

Type of contract	One day	Seasonal	Task work	Piece-work	Salaried	total
Percent	2.09	9.79	54.54	25.17	8.39	100

Source: 1982 Survey

There is also a slight difference in the incomes of the two groups of labourers, as was noted above, and is indicated in detail in table 3.10.

Table 3.10: Farm labourers: household income and income of household head (£S p.a.)

Category	average household income (£S)	average income of household head
All labourers	1 181	821
Arab labourers	1 193	857
Fellata labourers	1 115	719

Source: 1982 Survey

None of the three groups - average tenants, Arab labourers, Fellata labourers - has much more than their labour to sell on the market in order to gain their subsistence.

Curiously enough, it is the tenants who are the least 'free' in their relation to the labour markets, being encumbered by the obligations of the tenancy in return for a degree of security (the access to a dura crop) which is in part at least illusory given the fact that so many enter into sharecropping arrangements in just this crop. The situation is further complicated by the 'semi-organised' nature of the labour camp workers. This was noted by a number of observers from the 1940s to the present day, as well as the present study.[12] There is, of course, a range of actual contracts from the straightforward individual-to-individual contract for piecework to the complex sharecropping plus cash arrangement. But in general, the going rate is well known in the labour villages, and it is certainly in their interests not to enter into competition with each other either as individuals or villages, even though they may compete with labourers from the Arab villages. That this is the situation is indisputable; that the Fellata and Burgo are loth to admit it is to be expected. In the course of discussions with inhabitants of some labour camp villages in 1982, the issue was raised, and met with hasty denials. This is predictable, given the minority positions of the migrant labourers in the area, and their feeling that they are in a potentially insecure and unstable position as a population which is at least in part actually 'foreign' often having other than Sudanese nationality, and certainly culturally different.

We can summarise this section by saying that the inhabitants of the labour camp villages enter the market with the advantage that their work is necessary and in demand for tasks which must be done speedily. They can therefore drive a hard bargain, using their communal distinctiveness as part of that mechanism. But, this communal distinctiveness also means that they are vulnerable at the level of stereotype and ideology, and that this may also weaken their bargaining position, for it reflects the conflict in material interests between them and the tenants and the village labourers.

The migrant labourers

In the season 1980/81, a large number of labourers were imported by the Sudan Gezira Board to the irrigated area to enable the harvest of cotton to take place. This was in addition to those who had come alone. These labourers were recruited to 'rescue' those blocks which were reportedly short of labour. They came from various parts of the Sudan, distributed as follows:

Table 3.11: Distribution of labourers by area of origin

Area of origin	Number	Per cent
White Nile	24 359	64.61
North Kordofan	8 915	25.48
Gedaref	1 716	4.90
Total	34 990	99.99

Source: SGB: Survey of Labour Camps, 1979

Unfortunately, the research on which the present report is based was done in October, prior to the arrival of migrant labourers in the Gezira for the cotton harvest. It was not possible in the time available to visit these people in their home areas. Such research should be an urgent priority for anyone wishing to investigate this important aspect of the Sudanese economy.

The background 'push factors' which led people to migrate, have been dealt with schematically in Section II, and will be returned to briefly in Section V. The irrigated area still continues to draw labour from a wide catchment area, including not only Darfur and Kordofan but even Chad to the west, as well as from the southern provinces and from among refugee populations.[13] To a large extent such labourers have similar characteristics to the migrants described in the previous chapter.

Each December the Sudan Gezira Board forecasts its labour requirements for the cotton harvest. The need for labour additional to that from the Gezira is met in three ways:

(a)   Some tenants, usually in groups, travel to Southern Darfu, E. Kordofan, and also to other areas nearer to the Gezira. Often they travel to areas with which they have longstanding ties.

(b)   The SGB sets up picking labour committees jointly with the tenants and the government in different provinces.

(c)   Self-recruited labour which acts on the basis of information passed by word of mouth concerning likely demand and wage rates.

The majority of these labourers come to do agricultural work, predominantly picking, and their contract of employment is usually some variant of piecework and payment in kind.

The kinds of differentiation among the migrant labourers and the basis of their calculations in the wage bargain are outlined in the next section.

V.   Closing the bargain: labourers' calculations and
     imputed wage levels

As was discussed in the previous section, the tenants are not homogeneous. They are differentiated in a number of ways, most relevantly in terms of their wealth, social status and income, all of which distinguish between them in terms of their resources when they are entering into a bargain with labourers. The nature of the bargain and its outcome is also influenced by seasonal factors. We can examine these seasonal factors as they influence the labour bargain throughout the agricultural year.

(a) The picking labour recruitment season (November/December). At this stage the cotton crop is fairly well advanced, and the tenants have some idea of what kind of crop will be produced. They have a rough idea of how much labour they will require, and also of the level of wage they will be prepared to pay. 'Wage' is, of course, not precisely accurate given that the bargain with pickers often covers a range of arrangements from purely cash payment per guffa, payment of subsistence, housing, transport, a wage and often a 'balash' payment in addition.

Even in the home region, there will be some peasants who are ready and willing to migrate to the Gezira because of the impending 'dead' season in their own farming year. They will have the following information available to them on deciding whether and on what terms to make the journey: they will know something of the preceding year of years' wages trends; they may have certain 'targets' of cash that they want to earn in order to satisfy certain needs that they have; they may have an idea from other nearby communities, or from travellers, of the level of wages which is likely to be forthcoming the present season; depending on their knowledge of the availability of wage employment other than in the irrigated area, they are likely to have an idea of what the fare which either they or the tenant pays (or the SGB) is worth in terms of the access it may give them to other employment.

(b) During the picking season: the labourers can assume that the tenant will want maximum quantities picked, as will the picker, who is paid by the guffa. (These two aims are not always in accord - the picker wants to pick as much as possible per unit of time, the tenant has the additional factor of maximising per unit of area as well - in short, the picker may concentrate on the parts of the howasha where cotton is most dense, neglecting the sparser areas which are all marginal increments to the tenant.) These are the basic assumptions

which enter into the bargain during the picking season. Further
criteria depend on the type of tenant.

For simplicity, we can assume two main types of tenant
household: one wealthy and entrepreneurial, and the other a poor
tenant with little or no household labour. In the first case, it is
very likely that the tenant will act in a way consistent with the
model, in part because each marginal increment to cotton picked will
constitute an increase in net profit. This is even more likely to be
the case under the newly introduced individual account system which
assumes that all tenants ought to be able to act in this way.

In the second case, it is likely or at least possible that by
this time, the tenant will be fairly heavily in debt both to the SGB
and to local shopkeepers and perhaps even labourers by the beginning
of the picking season. If not irredeemably in debt, he or she will
at best be facing a serious cash-flow crisis. Picking advances will
be used at least in part for subsistence purposes. Faced with these
constraints, the tenant is unlikely to purchase labour up to the
margin. Indeed, their eyes may tell them that they already have a
low yield (perhaps because of inadequate weeding, insufficient
irrigation or a number of other reasons) due to inadequate financing
earlier in the season. In such circumstances, they have to decide
whether to sacrifice a part of their already meagre current
consumption in order to achieve the minimum production level or
break-even under the new individual account, 3 <u>kantars</u> per feddan.
(If they do this, they will in any case receive no return, or perhaps
a marginal one.) The alternative is to aim to pick a bare minimum,
sacrificing little of their consumption, avoiding debts to shopkeepers
to finance the pickers, but instead getting into debt to the SGB.
The question is at that stage (October) hypothetical.

The last strategy could be preferable for tenants because it
would not mean sacrificing current consumption and it would not
increase their debts to the local merchants.

The latter in turn implies that tenants would not have to share their _dura_ ahead of the coming season and they could safeguard a local line of credit. Furthermore, debts to the SGB are remote, and have at various times been 'suspended', 'written off', 'rescheduled'. Thus the tenants are aware that they are not alone in their debt to the SGB, and tend to adopt a 'hope for the best' attitude. In relation to these circumstances within which the tenant is operating and making his or her decisions, the picking labourers who have come from outside the scheme can adopt a number of strategies. Some pickers will use the advances that they have received for travel to make the journey to the irrigated area, but will then be attracted by other employment, either because it offers better payment or better working conditions or living conditions - for example in the Ginneries at Meringan or Hassaheisa. In a sense, such labourers appear as 'free' labourers at such a time because they are apparently responding to market forces at a time of effective labour shortage. The migrants who respond in this way tend to be the younger, unattached men who are probably also target workers. By contrast, the majority of the migrants who come to the irrigated areas are not 'free' individuals in this sense. They are not free insofar as they often have quite long-standing relationships with their employers - occasionally they may even have marriage relationships with their employers' families, although the impression is that this is nowadays relatively rare. In any case, such labourers have a range of non-market ties with their potential employers. This may be based on many years of association with one or more tenant households. In some cases, these links will have been in existence for a generation or more.

Next, we examine the behaviour and expectations of the picking labourers in a little more detail. What they are looking for is a degree of certainty about a number of features of their contract. These include living conditions, target earnings and the certainty that the employer will actually pay them on time.

These elements in their calculation mean that they are most likely to offer their services to the wealthier tenants who will not face problems of liquidity at a crucial period. Such tenants are used to running a large household and in all probability a number of enterprises in addition to their tenancy. Given this basis, the addition of a few migrant labourers to the existing household for a few months will result in neither financial nor organisational stress.

A third group of labourers may also be identified. These are those who come to a particular village, but not to a particular household and work for a number of tenants in turn. While such an arrangement may be satisfactory, it does have some degree of uncertainty attaching to it, insofar as different employers from the group will have varying resource endowments. Thus there may be variations in pay and living and working conditions during the working months. Given these features, labourers may adopt a strategy of working particularly hard for one of the employing households in order to gain a more exclusive contract for the next season.

This last comment draws our attention to the possibility of a migrant career cycle. What this might consist of is not clear at present, and would require further data. However, some of the elements for its analysis would be:

(a)   the migrant household cycle;

(b)   the agricultural cycle in the labour sending area;

(c)   climatic features such as desertification and drought;

(d)   the tendency of new kinds of agricultural production, such as mechanised farming, to encroach on traditional rainfed agriculture.

We can look briefly at each of these, although no conclusions are currently possible.

(a)   The migrant household cycle: Two broad types of migrant labourer may be distinguished. The first group consists of the young,

unmarried men who come during the 'slack' season.[14]   Their aim in
making the journey may be to earn cash for specific purposes, in
particular to accumulate cash towards marriage payments or to
accumulate a small capital for small-scale trading purposes or, in
some cases, to pay school fees.   Such workers can be assumed to be
relatively mobile between employers at their destination.   They will
also be relatively responsive to wage differentials, for their aim is
to make the largest possible amount of money in the period that they
spend in the irrigated areas.   They are also to some degree
time-flexible, perhaps not being the only or main labour resource on
the household farm in their area of origin.

The second type of migrant labourer is the family, travelling as
a unit.   They also travel in their own 'slack season'.   In the
calculations of this type of labour unit, security of living
conditions and consistent availability of work will be of greater
importance than for the first group.   For this reason, they are
probably less money responsive, valuing other elements of the wages
contract.   The reason why such household groups make the journey is
because their traditional agriculture does not provide them with
sufficient to meet all their needs at the level of life to which they
aspire or require as a basic survival minimum.   Given the low
prevailing wage rates, it is likely that the income of such labourers
does not allow much more than bare economic survival.   The 1982
survey that the average cotton picking daily wage rates were £S1.86
for men and £S1.27 for women, for 59 observations.   About half of
these cases referred to migrant labourers.   As there is no minimum
wages legislation in relation to migrant labourers (and it is
difficult to see how there could be), it is possible that they are in
fact only subsisting, while little or nothing of their earnings
actually returns to their areas of origin.

(b) The crop cycle: We know that the cropping pattern in the Western
areas of the Sudan has peaks of labour demand.   These are different
from those in the irrigated areas.   What we do not know are the
details of labour demand and labour availability within this crop

cycle.   It would, in addition, be most useful to have information on
the variations in length of the growing season and yields over a ten-
or twenty-year period.   Such information, together with further
details of yield variation, would enable us to identify more clearly
the nature of the push factors which induce people to migrate.

(c) Desertification: The Western Sudan has been affected over the
past twelve years by the apparent changes in climate which are evident
across the whole Sahelian Zone.   Further information on this would
allow us to distinguish between natural processes which create push
factors, such as those indicated in (b) above, and man-made processes,
such as lack of investment and encroachment on non-capital intensive
systems of agriculture by capital-intensive profit-oriented systems.

(d) Encroachment on traditional areas: This process is related to
(b) and (c) above, for the encroachment of mechanised agriculture will
undoubtedly result in some areas in a diminution of the area available
for traditional rainfed cultivation through limitation of the land
area and soil mis-use.   This in turn may result in processes of
desertification, decreasing fallows and falling productivity.   Thus,
the agricultural year will become shorter and the harvest will
decline.   The evidence that this process is in train is uneven and
sparse.   Simpson and Simpson (1978) indicate that there are ambiguous
effects.   In some cases, mechanised farming is certainly decreasing
the area available to traitional rainland techniques, in others, the
presence of tractors for hire may have actually increased the area
cultivated by some of the wealthier traditional cultivators.   In the
Nuba mountain area, the process is equally mixed, although this mixed
nature may indicate a more general tendency.   As mechanised farming
in this area has developed, some villages have become isolated from
their tradition lands, and the rotation has shortened.   In the
opinion of one researcher, the tendency is for traditionally rainfed
agriculture to decline, and for the local farmers to become local wage
labourers on the mechanised schemes or to go as migrants to other
areas.[16]

We now turn to a consideration of the wages of Arab and Fellata labourers. The following three tables indicate the wage levels which can be imputed from tenants' reports of their costs. These figures must be treated with caution, as representing orders of magnitude only. They are not entirely representative of actual wages, particularly with regard to the harvest and post harvest operations, where a large element of non-monetary payment is usually involved in the contract.

Table 3.12: Imputed daily wages for men and women by crop operation for dura cultivation

Dura	Men: Average daily wage (£S)	Women: Average daily wage (£S)
Crop operation		
Land preparation	2.64	
Planting	2.19	1.46
Replanting	1.86	
Weeding	2.10	1.50
Fertilizer application	3.00	
Irrigation	1.95	
Harvest	2.33	
Mean: all operations	2.17	1.28

Source: 1982 Survey

Table 3.13: Imputed daily wage for men and women by crop operation, for cotton cultivation

Cotton	Men: Daily wage (£S)	Women: Daily wage (£S)
Crop operation		
Land preparation	3.02	1.33
Planting	2.11	0.99
Replanting	2.24	2.00
Weeding	2.15	2.47
Fertilizer application	2.55	
Pesticide application	2.13	
Irrigation	1.90	
Harvest	1.86	1.27
Post harvest	1.77	1.95
Mean: all operations	2.18	1.60

Source: 1982 Survey

Table 3.14: Imputed daily wge for men and women by crop operation for groundnuts cultivation

Groundnuts	Men: Daily wage (£S)	Women: Daily wage (£S)
Crop operation		
Land preparation	3.04	
Planting	1.67	1.00
Replanting	1.13	
Weeding	1.89	2.50
Irrigation	0.62	
Harvest	1.96	
Post harvest	2.05	
Mean: all operations	1.95	1.75

Source: 1982 Survey

What is immediately apparent from these tables is that women make a notable contribution to all crops, but in particular to cotton, where they are involved in all the major operations.

Table 3.15: Mean imputed wages of men and women by crop

Crop	Male average imputed wage (£S) per day	Female average imputed wage (£S) per day
Cotton	2.18	1.60
Dura	2.17	1.28
Groundnuts	1.95	1.75

Source: 1982 Survey

This being said, it is clear that this difference in picking wage rates for men and women which has already been noted, is generally the case. The exception is for the weeding operation which is usually said to be a 'woman's' job, where the imputed average daily wage would seem to be higher for women than for men for both cotton and groundnuts.

VI. The economic viability of tenancies

From the viewpoint of the tenants' private profitability, the tendency provides a low return, both to area and to labour. The evidence for this is now very clear. Two sources can be adduced to support the statement. The Annual Report of Field Crop Economic Survey, 1980/81[17] shows that for long staple cotton growers, the next financial return per feddan (total revenue per feddan - total cost per feddan) was -£S3.941. Only by assuming (a) that the tenants' household labour received payments of £S20.330 per feddan (which would only be true in some cases) and (b) that £S11.50 per feddan was received from the stabilisation fund, was a net economic return per feddan of £S16.389 arrived at.[18] The situation for growers of Acala cotton is similar. The net financial return per feddan was £S3.843, including a payment of £S17.50 per feddan from the stabilisation fund, and also assuming payment of £S20.330 per feddan to household labour. Without these assumptions, the real return to the tenant would have been - £S33.987 per feddan.

The second piece of evidence that the tenancy is unprofitable for the tenant is received from the report by the Ministry of Finance and Economic Planning, <u>Study of Cost of Production and Comparative Advantage of Crops in Sudan</u>, May 1982.[19] At average 1980/81 yields, the mean private profit for ELS cotton in Gezira was calculated as - £S45.07 per feddan and for Acala - £S41.22. Even at a high yield level, ELS only gave a profit of £S4.60 per feddan and Acala still made a loss at - £S9.90 per feddan.

To get some idea of the financial situation of a tenancy taking account of all crops, the average net income per tenancy was calculated using data from the SGB report and from the IBRD. These calculations are shown in Tables 3.16 and 3.17.

There is clearly a great divergence in the results, although both surveys are based on random sampling methods. Why this should be the case is difficult to explain. However, even on the more favourable figures, those of the SGB, the annual agricultural household income for a tendency of ten feddans was about £S460, and for a five-feddan tenancy about £S230. As an indication of the level of income which might serve as a comparison for that of the tenants, the Euroconsult Report notes that "Tenants' incomes should range between that of an unskilled labourer and that of a skilled labourer, i.e. between £S600 and £S1,625." This range was that payable to skilled labourers by the SGB during the 1981 season. Quite clearly, even under the most optimistic estimates available, those of the SGB, where an element of cash payment to household labour is assumed, the income from a tenancy is well below this target. However, the present survey found a mean <u>agricultural</u> income for tenants' households of about £S747 (the SGB figure is for 1980-81, the survey dealt with 1981-82), which is larger

Table 3.16: Tenancy income estimates using SGB figures as bases

Cropping pattern	Total net income 10 feddans cotton (£S)	Total net income 5 feddans cotton (£S)
1. ELS + Dura and ground-nuts (sharecropped)	450.94	225.47
2. ELS + Dura + groundnuts (household labour)	528.82	264.41
3. ELS + Dura + Wheat	287.89	143.95
4. MS + Dura + groundnuts (sharecropped)	525.76	262.88
5. MS + Dura + groundnuts (household labour)	603.69	301.69
6. MS + Dura + wheat	362.76	181.38
Average	459.99	229.96

Source: SGB 1981.

Note: These figures assume: (1) household labour is paid by the household head, and that this money thus forms part of household income. (2) £S11.50 per feddan is received from the stabilisation fund.

Table 3.17: Gezira tenancy income estimates using IBRD Figures as bases

Cropping pattern	Total net income (£S) 10 feddans cotton	Total net income (£S) 5 feddans cotton
1. ELS + Dura + groundnuts	-370.84	-185.42
2. ELS + Dura + wheat	-450.37	-225.18
3. MS + Dura + groundnuts	-332.32	-166.16
4. MS + Dura + groundnuts	-411.87	-205.43
Average net income	-391.14	-195.67

Source: IBRD 1982.

Note: The IBRD figures do not provide a basis of calculation which takes into account sharecropping.

than the SGB estimate for a ten-feddan cotton tenancy. The range of values was, however, very large, from £S2 to £S5,242. In contrast total household income was much higher with a mean of £S2,304, but once again with a large range, from £S180 to £S14,152. The actual level of tenants' agricultural income remains uncertain, but what is clear is that they are comparatively low.

The following table shows mean agricultural income for households with cotton holdings of 6 feddans or less, and for holdings of between 10 and 20 feddans of cotton as indicated by the 1982 survey.

Table 3.18:   Cotton area and mean agricultural income

Cotton area (feddans)	Mean agricultural income (£S)
Less than 6 feddans	550
10 - 20 feddans	2,129

Source: 1982 Survey

If we look at the total household income for the two groups, we find the following:

Table 3.19:   Cotton area by mean total household income

Cotton area (feddans)	Urban total household income (£S)
Less than 6 feddans	1,829
10-20 feddans	2,765

Source: 1982 Survey.

Only 30 per cent of their household income comes from their tenancy, the remaining 70 per cent coming from other activities. If we further consider that the proportion of the agricultural income deriving from cotton is likely to be very small indeed, then the implications are disturbing. Table 3.2 above shows that the percentage of total labour in person days per feddan consumed by cotton is 52.80 per cent of all labour inputs; and that cotton consumes 59.16 per cent of all non-household labour inputs to all crops. The moral is easy to draw. The tenants must enquire whether the return merits the expenditure of their time, effort and their money. From the viewpoint of this study, this must affect their willingness to participate enthusiastically in agricultural work, and thus their ability and willingness to employ labour. Insofar as they are bound to employ labour in any case in order to justify their continued occupation of the tenancy, the probable effects are to push them into various forms of debt and to encourage them to direct their efforts, wherever possible, into other forms of income-earning activity.

VII. Policy recommendations

Following from this analysis, what then are the conclusions and policy recommendations which might be derived? With regard to the refugee population of the Eastern and Southern Sudan, there is little which can be directly derived from the present study in the short term. However, in the longer term, the following recommendations could, under the right conditions, create a demand for labour which would offer additional employment opportunitites to many members of the Sudanese population, including the refugees.

From the evidence presented in this study, the fundamental issue which has to be confronted within the irrigated areas is that of the optimal crop mix. Related to this is the additional question of the relations of production.

Cotton seems to be beset by two problems. One is its low level of profitability for almost 75 per cent of the Gezira population; the other is its secular decline in yield over the last twenty years. These two characteristics may not be unrelated, and may indeed reflect the unwillingness of tenants to allocate their labour and financial resources to its cultivation when their experience teaches them that the returns to their labour and to their capital from this crop are low. An important indicator that this is the case is that the Fellata will specifically not enter into sharecropping agreements in relation to cotton, whereas they will do so with alacrity where dura, groundnuts or wheat are concerned. As representatives of the 'free' wage labour in the scheme, it must be assumed that they are acting rationally in the allocation of their labour in relation to the various crops which are grown.

In recent seasons, the SGB has begun to 'cut out' cotton from the rotation of some tenants, largely for reasons of inadequate water supply and/or unsuitable soils. It is the recommendation of this report that far larger areas of cotton should be cut out from the rotation, in order that only the most efficient tenants, and those with adequate capital available, should continue to cultivate the crop. In a sense, the new individual account system is a step on the road towards this reappraisal of the crop mix in the Scheme. Information about the percentage of tenants breaking even or making profits under the new arrangements are as yet unclear. However, certain information is available to indicate the order of magnitude of tenants breaking even or making a profit.

The SGB survey of a representative sample of tenants in the 1980/81 season showed that "none of the tenants growing Acala cotton had benefited from the progressive production incentive policy" and that "only 8.5 per cent of tenants growing long staple cotton had benefited from the incentive programme".[21] In addition, interviews with research staff of the SGB indicated that in the 1981-82 season, 55 per cent of tenants made a profit, and 16 per cent of them made more than £S500.00 from a ten feddan tenancy. The actual size of the profit which accrued to the 55 per cent is not clear. What is clear is, as has been stated above, that the crop is certainly marginal for a very large number of tenants.

This being the case, the implication is that they would prefer not to grow cotton, and that their economic use of the imported inputs to cotton cultivation is likely to be low or even negative. For medium staple cotton, "the most notable feature ... is that at low levels of productivity, i.e. for yields up to 1.5 kantars per feddan, it consumes more foreign exchange than it earns and this disadvantage is relatively greater under pump irrigation". And, as regards international competitiveness, at low productivity levels "all crops under all types of farming, except rainfed traditional sesame, are non-competitive while medium staple cotton and wheat even have negative coefficients". For long staple cotton, at both low and medium levels of productivity, there is a considerable loss for the farmer and its level of foreign exchange dependence is high, at 80 per cent.[22]

Most tenants certainly do not consider the cotton crop as being 'theirs': they have long made the distinction between 'their' dura and the government's cotton. They could be relieved of some part of what is nothing less than a burden for many of them, andd so at the same time relieve the Sudanese economy of a portion of the foreign exchange requirements for the fertilizer and chemicals needed to grow the crop.

The Gezira Scheme and the other irrigated areas could be zoned with regard to suitability in relation to soils and ease of watering, into those areas where cotton should be grown and those where it should not. Within these areas, the wealthier, better endowed farmers should be encouraged to continue cotton cultivation. And they should be supported by intensive extension and agronomic advice. These farmers do not at present face any labour shortage, and with the removal of competition for labour at peak periods, they would be very unlikely to face it in the future.

The remaining tenants could then be offered the opportunity to cultivate a mixture of vegetables, dura and groundnuts on their tenancies. Such an arrangement could provide adequate staple supplies for the Gezira population, and hopefully, a marketable surplus which

would not be <u>sheiled</u> to the same extent as at present, some of the
tenants having been relieved of the necessity of cultivating cotton.
Vegetables appear to be a profitable crop in the Gezira and most
successfully cultivated by a number of Fellata in the survey who
reported high incomes from their sale. Not only is there a ready
urban market within reach, but also, and most importantly, the
possibility of air-freighting of produce to the Gulf should be
explored.

The third crop, groundnuts, is included in this scenario for a
number of reasons. Under Gezira conditions, its level of foreign
exchange dependence is low at 43 per cent.[23] Its private
profitability is also positive, although not as high as wheat. The
latter, however, has a very high level of foreign exchange
dependence. It could therefore recoup some of the foreign exchange
loss by lowering the area devoted to cotton, and also provide cash
income. However, another reason for increasing the area sown to
groundnuts would be to ensure a continued and even expanded role in
the Scheme for the Fellata who already extensively sharecrop in this
crop, and who in a few cases have rights to land for its cultivation.
They, as has been indicated above, have made, and continue to make, a
major contribution to the labour supply in the area. These policy
recommendations refer essentially to the viability of individual
tenant cultivation on the Gezira scheme. It is important to note that
they will inevitably be constrained by the macro-economic requirements
of the whole economy, such as Sudan's urgent need for foreign
exchange. Thus the degree to which such policies can be implemented
depends crucially on the economic balances which are involved in the 6
Year Plan and which are the basis for planners' decisions. For
present purposes the possibility of such overall macro-economic
feasibility is assumed, even though it cannot be taken for granted.
This assumption allows for the most bold policy suggestions, which may
be the extreme limit of actual policy choices. Somewhat less extreme
policy choices may also have a positive impact, in terms of partial
restructuring of the irrigated schemes' production pattern.

It could be predicted that were such a policy to be implemented, requiring as it does a basic reappraisal of the cropping strategy and organisational infrastructure of the area, then there would be major effects on the demand for labour. The following adjustments are foreseeable:

(i) a drop in the overall demand for picking labour, thus reduced migration from the traditional areas of origin of this labour;

(ii) an ironing out of the major peaks in the cultivation season, and thus in the competition among tenants for labour at current peak periods;

(iii) an increase in the use of household labour, as the profitability of the new crop mix encourages households to cultivate their land themselves.

Insofar as for a short time at least, the local labourers, both Arab and Fellata, might face a decline in the demand for their services, a minimum agricultural wages policy would have to be considered, in order to ensure that they do not suffer a s a result of the change. However, in the longer term, this would probably be unecessary, for the following reasons:

(i) vegetable growing is labour intensive, and if it expanded, and tenants see the benefits to be derived from intensive production, so the demand for local labour would be likely to rise;

(ii) the growing of vegetables should create new employment opportunities in the area, associated with the processing, transporting and packing of vegetables;

(iii) the dura areas and the groundnut areas could be expanded, in place of cotton, and these two crops together would continue to require heavy labour input.

An additional reason for minimum wages legislation would be to ensure that some of the benefits of the new strategy would accrue to migrant labourers who came to the Scheme, and that these benefits are thus transferred back to their areas of origin. However, overall, it is likely that the level of remittances to these areas of White Nile, Kordofan and Darfur Provinces would inevitably decline. This may not be a bad thing. Labour migration places stress on both the individuals who undertake it and on those who are left behind. In addition, it is also likely to contribute to the decline of rainfed agriculture in the West. The implication of this is that an attempt should be made to invest in minimum tillage and other improvement techniques in the Western Sudan, similar to those currently being experimented with in the Savannah Development Project, Phase II. Such improvements could halt, and even reverse the decline of agriculture in these areas, and given the low foreign exchange dependence of groundnuts, dura, millet and sesame grown under those conditions, expansion and improvement of production would benefit the Sudanese economy in general.

There is another issue which should be considered, which is that of the employment possibilities for the new generation growing up in the irrigated areas. Subdivision of holdings has now occurred to such an extent that it is difficult to see how further subdivision could accommodate the rising population. The solution to this problem requires careful planning - it is unlikely that the solution lies in employing those young people on their parents' tenancies, or on their being able to become tenants in their own right.

The answer probably lies in a complete reconceptualisation of the role and nature of the irrigated area. This would be consonant with the view put forward in the first part of these recommendations. Were the irrigated areas to become the focus of an agro-industrial complex, then the region could conceivably become a major source of new employment, which might stem the tendency of young people to migrate to the urban areas and keep them satisfactorily employed in their home areas.

It is not inconceivable that such development could also provide employment opportunities for refugees in the longer term. The transformation of the irrigated areas into a mixture of intensive and efficient cash cropping of efficiently produced and readily marketable vegetables and fruits, supported by a relevant small-scale horticultural technology and extension services, together with allied processing industries should be a source of increased employment in the area, and of improved food security and higher export for the Sudan as a whole.

Footnotes

[1] One sample village was in the White Nile Corporation area near Dueim.

[2] Source: ILO 1982 Survey 2.

[3] These are arbitrary cut-off points, but the general principle is that a newly-established household has only two units of labour available; a "mature" household has two adults together with children; and an elderly household may once again be reduced to two adults who, in this case, may be unable to undertake a heavy work load.

[4] A. Abdel Hamid (1966) pp. 103, 104 et passim.

[5] Abdalla El Amin and Ahmed Elbedawi, Annual Report of Field Crops Economic Surveys: Season 1980-81. SGB, Barakat 1981, pp. 4-6, 17-18, 27-29.

[6] S.A. Ahmed (1977), pp. 203-205.

[7] ibid., pp. 99, 109, 113-118, 136.

[8] These are discussed in more detail in the following section.

[9] The following paragraph is based on J.D. Tothill (1948) and P.M. Holt (1958).

[10] Sudan Gezira Board (1979, Arabic).

[11] Thus, Nur Ali Suleiman (1952), Ahmed Abdel Hamid (1966), G. Brausch, J. Crooks and D.J. Shaw (1964).

[12] E.g. Tothill (1948), Brausch et. al. (1964) and Barnett (1978).

[13] See ILO (1976) p. 96.

[14] It should be noted that the "slack season" is not a variable determined by tradition alone. It is also affected (increasingly) by climatic features as well as the impact of new forms of cultivation on traditional rural systems.

[15] Personal communication to A. Barnett from Abdalla al Hassan.

[16] Thus Affan (1978) states that an area of 25,000 feddans was taken by the Habila Scheme in South Kordofan, displacing around 850 families. Most of these people were believed to have moved southwards to the Nuba mountains.

[17] El Amin and Elbedawi (1981).

[18] This figure appears at £S16.092 in the report. It appears to have been miscalculated.

[19] IBRD (1982).

[20] Euroconsult (1982), p. 61.

[21] Elamin and Elbedawi (1981), p. 47.

[22] IBRD (1982), pp. 32, 51-55, et passim.

[23] Ibid. p. 39.

APPENDIX   TO CHAPTER 3:

A Note on Labour Migration from Nueila Village

The sample showed a total of 23 adult men as having left the village in order to look for work.   This is about 5.7 per cent of the sample population, and represents about 100 men from the whole village.   Given a male population aged 16 years or more, of about 442, then around 22.6 per cent of that population has at some time left the village in search of work.

In discussion with the elders of one section of the village, it was apparent that many men were currently absent working abroad, mainly in the Gulf States or Saudi Arabia, although one or two were in Libya.   The village elders estimated that about 100 men were away, and reported the following distribution of occupations among those young men absent from their section of the village (probably about 25 per cent of the total village population):

Builders	6	
Blacksmiths	2	
Carpenters	2	
Drivers	2	
Labourers	15	
Decorators	2	
Office workers	1	
Soldiers	3	(in the Abu Dhabi army)
Mechanics	2	

In view of the these figures, the elders were asked if this meant that there was a shortage of skilled men in the village now.   The general opinion was that this was not so.   There still remained in the village 50 builders, 4 carpenters, 6 blacksmiths and 3 mechanics.

The effects of remittances from these migrant workers was evident. A second mosque had been built since 1978, several new brick houses were under construction, and there were more vehicles in evidence than in 1978. All these things, the villagers said were the result of remittances from migrant workers. An additional effect of these remittances is that some few tenants are in effect subsidising the work of their tenancies from the remittances they receive from family members employed in other countries. A total of 28 household heads (17.28 per cent of the total sample) reported receiving remittances from household members working in town or abroad. These remittances were distributed as follows:

Table A1: <u>Value of annual remittances (£S) to households</u>

Range (£S)	Number	Percentage
1 - 199	11	39.28
200 - 999	12	42.86
1 000 - 5 000	5	17.86
<u>Total</u>	28	100.0

Minimum value: £S.15
Mean value: £S.630
Maximum value: £S4,800
<u>Source</u>: 1982 Survey

The possibility that such remittances perpetuate certain forms of production or allow for the economic viability of households, conforms to the pattern, evident from the following chapter, in the urban economy. This has important implications for the future if avenues for migrant workers dry up as they appear to be doing.

PART III:

THE URBAN SECTOR

Contributor:

Jayati Ghosh

CHAPTER 4

Urban Labour Markets

I.   Introduction

This chapter adopts a dynamic perspective.   The emphasis is not
on the static allocation of labour resources within the urban economy
so much as on the dynamic effects on urban labour markets of the
growing "internationalisation" of the Sudanese economy and other
macro-economic processes.

These processes, which were outlined in Chapter 1, include the
high rates of rural-urban migration in the recent past[1] which have
not been matched by a concomitant increase in urban industrial
employment.   This has implied an increase both in disguised
unemployment and underemployment and in non-organised sector
employment in urban areas.   At the same time, the recent substantial
labour emigration to oil-exporting countries has affected not only
remittances and the internal demand structure, but also the labour
market.   The effects of emigration are discussed in greater detail in
a later section.

The indirect effects of emigration as well as the overall
stagnation of the economy which was described in the first chapter,
affect the nature of urban employment by differentiating between the
degree of viability of various urban economic activities.   These can
be broadly classified into the following groups.

(1) Declining - those areas of industry facing shrinking demand,
    competition from imports, or the need to compete in the export
    market: such as textiles and leather products.

(2) Stagnating - those areas with no shortage of demand, but where
    supply constraints prevent full capacity utilisation: such as
    sugar, food processing and cement production.

(3) Expanding - those areas where the increase in demand is so great that operations are profitable in spite of supply constraints: such as construction, transport, hotels and restaurants and other services. Many of these activities come in the range of "informal sector" employment.

The differences between these types of urban economic activities have major effects on the remuneration for different kinds of work and the terms and conditions of employment, as is argued in later sections.

Most of the empirical material used in this chapter is based on a survey conducted in Greater Khartoum, Kenana and Port Sudan in August and September 1982. The three conurbations together account for slightly more than half of the total urban population of the Sudan.[2] The survey, which used a household questionnaire applied to workers (and some unemployed) in factories, workshops, construction areas, market places, etc., was purposive rather than random in nature. The aim was to cover as many types of urban labour as possible, rather than get a strictly representative sample of the urban population. Thus the data cannot be used for statistical inference: however, it does provide fairly detailed information on wages, working conditions, incomes and pattern of migration for different types of workers' households. The survey covered a total of 807 households - 446 in the three towns of greater Khartoum, 75 in Kenanan and 285 in Port Sudan - including a total of 4,552 persons. A smaller, individual, survey of migrants leaving to work abroad was taken at the Passport, Emigration and Labour Office and the Saudi Arabian Embassy, all in Khartoum. This provided a set of information regarding 216 migrants.

In addition to the survey data, this chapter also uses material gathered through interviews with employers, officials and trade unionists over the same two-month period in the Sudan. Some use was also made of published material. The data base on urban labour in Sudan is extremely limited and the quality rather dubious. Available statistics on aspects such as the numbers in the urban workforce,

Data problem

employment modes and payment for work are scanty; and methods of
collection frequently leave much to be desired. Furthermore, there
is no data on investment or wage trends, among other things. Thus,
such published data as are used are presented for purposes of
comparison rather than for their strict reliability.

The chapter begins with a schematic categorisation of the main
urban labour markets and their relation to the rural markets for
labour. The next section covers the nature, causes and effects of
one of the most important economic phenomena in recent times: the
relatively large-scale emigration of labour, mainly to the Arab
oil-exporting countries. The markets for skilled and unskilled
labour are discussed in sections IV and V. Section VI highlights
some specific features in both subsectors. These are primarily
related to various forms of market segmentation - sex differentiation,
regional spread, relation between type of employer and wages, etc.
In Section VII are considered the possibilities open to refugees given
the constraints of the labour market. Section VIII discusses the
role of the Government, labour legislation, minimum wage policies and
the functioning of the Labour Offices. The last section is devoted
to a synthesis of the features described earlier.

II. Characteristics of urban labour markets

The population of the Sudan, like that of most other developing
countries, is predominantly rural. Nevertheless, approximately
one-fourth of the country's population of about 18 million lives in
urban areas.[3] Of this number, about half live in Greater Khartoum
and Port Sudan. There are some other important urban areas, but none
to match these two in terms of size, extent of industrial activity and
volume of urban employment. These two urban conurbations thus
account for a significant proportion of the urban labour force as
well. The total labour force in Sudan in 1980 was estimated to be in
the region of 5.58 million, of which slightly more than one million
would be urban.[4]

This serves to give some idea of the dimensions of the object of study. The analysis of urban labour in the Sudan would refer ultimately to a shifting population of two to three million people; shifting, because of the high rates of internal and external migration in the Sudan. The fairly high concentration of population in Greater Khartoum and Port Sudan creates its own momentum, as it contributes to further rural–urban migration to these centres.[5] Furthermore, the two cities display the main feature of labour markets in all urban areas in the Sudan, so it is useful to take them as examples.

A preliminary typology of urban labour markets would include the following sectors: the Government and public sector, the organised private sector and the unorganised private sector. Within each of these there is further segmentation, primarily into groups such as professionals, white collar workers, skilled workers, semi-skilled and unskilled workers. There are also distinctions according to sex, region of origin, type of industry or activity, etc. These urban sectors of the labour market would operate in relation to, on the one hand, the international market which attracts Sudanese labour, and on the other hand, the main rural labour groups: traditional peasants, agricultural labourers, non-agricultural rural workers and nomadic pastoralists.

The Government and the public sector corporations are the major urban employers, accounting for slightly more than one quarter of all urban workers. Being the largest employers, they set the tone for organised private sector employment as well as the general basis for working conditions. It is significant that within the public sector the pay structure is not determined by market supply and demand forces but institutionally. There is an established hierarchy of pay grades, largely based on educational qualifications and length of service rather than on the exact type of work done.[6] This system of pay scales is revised every few years (recently in 1978 and thereafter in 1982) but the basic premises remain unchanged. Thus the system of payment for work in the public sector does not take into account shortages or surpluses of types of workers.

Furthermore, the Government, until some years ago, operated a system of guaranteed employment for graduates. This system, which was discontinued in 1974 for Arts graduates, in 1978 for Science graduates and in 1980 for Agriculture graduates, led to substantial overstaffing and underemployment in Government departments. It also had deleterious effects on manpower availability, because it affected the orientation of education and training. A university degree (usually in the liberal arts subjects) became the most coveted qualification for urban youth, because it guaranteed employment and resulted in relatively higher rates of pay. Thus technical and vocational training were de-emphasised, and the five universities of the Sudan produced large numbers of graduates who did not possess the training or skills required for development projects or industry.

Although the system of guaranteed employment has now been abolished, its effects in terms of a top-heavy administrative structure and substantial, disguised underemployment in the Government (and in some public sector corporations) are still being felt. Also, the educational structure has not displayed much flexibility in terms of adjusting to the changed employment conditions, and continues to churn out arts graduates who then have difficulty finding appropriate employment within the country.[7] There has been a tendency to downplay the acquisition of manual and technical skills and a preference for white-collar jobs - but this is being increasingly affected by the shortage of manual skills and the consequent increase in remuneration for them.

The fact that employment and wages in the Government and public sector are not determined by market considerations affects the nature of urban labour exchange in general. In the organised private sector, although demand and supply forces play important roles, the effect of Government employment policy is clearly felt in the labour market. The organised private sector is here used to refer to permanent workers in registered establishments of whatever size. It therefore includes basically all private sector workers who are covered by labour legislation, but not casual or daily paid workers

even if they work in organised industry. Within this latter group,
the wage structure tends to be more flexible and responsive to market
pressures. Nevertheless public sector wages do provide some sort of
guideline for wages in this sector. For example, in both Khartoum
and Port Sudan, it was found that the starting wages for unskilled
labour in the organised private sector tended to average around the
level of the public sector minimum wage, plus a premium. Thus, while
the Government minimum wage totalled £S40 per month (£S28 + £S12 for
transport) most factories in the Greater Khartoum area paid unskilled
labourers around £S45 per month as a starting wage.[8]

In this context, it is relevant to note that while labour
organisations and trade unions do exist within this sector, their
bargaining power is severely curtailed because of a ban on all
strikes. In most cases this has been respected and trade unions do
not do more than negotiate with employers over wages, working
conditions etc. (There are some prominent exceptions to this, such
as the railway workers' union in Atbara and the Co-operative Society
of Dockworkers in Port Sudan.) Wages are usually determined in
companies by "collective agreements" between representatives of the
workers and of the management, every two or three years. Since these
pay scales have some form of inflation index built in only in very
rare cases, they tend to become outdated fairly quickly, given the
very rapid rate of inflation.

The unorganised private sector of the urban workforce covers both
casual labour in organised industry and the various forms of labour
within the "informal sector" Casual, or daily or weekly paid,
labour tends to be quite important. For example, most firms in
Salabona, the industrial area in Port Sudan, tended to employ up to 50
per cent of their labour on a casual basis.[9] Such labour is also
important in Khartoum factories, albeit to a somewhat lesser extent.
In all urban areas it is the general rule for factories and other
companies that workers are first hired for a probation period of 3
months, during which they are treated as casual labour. Because of
the high turnover rates of labour,[10] many workers do not stay

long enough with one company to get beyond this casual status, and therefore remain in this "unorganised" group.

The informal sector refers to those self-employed or employed by private individuals, who are not subject to industrial or labour regulation. The difficulties in defining and analysing this group are immense, and often it is treated simply as the residual. An earlier study characterised the following features of the informal sector: ease of entry, reliance on indigenous sources, family or individual ownership of enterprises, small scale operation, labour intensive and adapted technology, skills adopted outside the formal education system and unregulated, competitive markets.[11] Some studies of the Greater Khartoum area have used self-employment as a proxy for the informal sector.[12] In this analysis, all those working for themselves or for private individuals are considered as part of the informal sector. In urban Sudan this form of employment covers a wide range of activities, from petty trading to services, including transport. The remuneration for work in this group is almost completely determined by market forces and varies with the state of economic activity. Entry and exit are easy in this labour market, and income can fluctuate substantially. In urban Sudan analysis of this sector is made more complex by the high and growing degree of overlap between it and the organised sector of employment, in that labour is very mobile between the two sectors; and the growing importance of subsidiary occupations means that many people may be working in both sectors. Employment in this sector reflects most directly particular tendencies at work in the economy: the ranks are swelled by rural-urban maigration, whether permanent or seasonal; and economically expanding sectors such as transport, construction, restaurants and cafés and other services speedily find labour.

This describes the main "static" features of urban labour markets in the main cities of the Sudan. In sum, the wage structure in the organised sector tends to be substantially affected by the principal employer - the Government - which does not operate according to supply/demand criteria. (Now, however, the growing shortage of skilled manual labour is forcing a change, and the discrepancy in wages between white collar and skilled manual work is speedily diminishing.)   The private sector, which contains both "organised" and "unorganised" elements, is growing in importance.   In the unorganised sector wages correspond generally to market conditions. Tables 4.2 and 4.4 below indicate the prevailing wage levels for a number of occupations.   There is substantial labour mobility, on three different levels: from the Sudan, abroad; from rural to urban areas; from employer to employer within particular urban areas. These three forms of labour mobility present a crucial aspect of urban labour markets, without which their functioning cannot be understood.

III. Labour emigration

Unlike some other labour-exporting countries, the Sudan does not have a long history of emigration for work.   The present flow of emigrants is part of a relatively recent phenomenon, reflecting in essence the increased demand for labour from the Arab oil-exporting countries.   Thus, large-scale movements of labour date principally from the late 1970s.

Originally such emigration was seen, both by the Sudanese Government and by external observers,[13] as providing net benefits to the economy through the bringing in of valuable foreign exchange, export of unemployment and acquisition by Sudanese working abroad of useful skills which could be exploited on their return.   However, this optimism has been largely belied by the experience of the last few years.   Labour export has been the cause of or accessory to a number of problems now confronting the Sudanese economy, and its beneficial impact appears to have been outweighed by the other effects which have, paradoxically, contributed to the present economic trough and persistent stagflation.

Although the numbers of Sudanese working abroad appear fairly small when compared with the volume of, for example, Asians working in Saudi Arabia and the Gulf countries, they are very large in relation to the labour force within the Sudanese economy. The official Labour Department list of Sudanese working abroad in 1981 totalled 330,260.[14] However, it is widely accepted that official emigration forms only a minor proportion of the total number of emigrant labourers. Galal El Din's (1978) study estimated that unrecorded migration could account for as much as 70-80 per cent of actual migration for work from the Sudan.[15] This means that the real number of Sudanese workers abroad could be between 1.1 to 1.6 million. Even if a more conservative estimate of an unofficial migration rate of two-thirds is taken, this still implies a total of one million Sudanese migrants for work abroad.

These numbers must be seen in relation to a total population of approximately 18 million, a labour force of around 5.58 million, and an urban workforce of little more than one million. Thus the number of Sudanese working abroad may even exceed the total urban labour force of the country. Even through all the migrants are not urban in origin, in all probability most of them would have resided in a city for at least some time before their departure from the Sudan. In any event they still represent a substantial withdrawal from the potential urban labour force.

There is a possiblity that the number of those leaving to work abroad may taper off in the near future. Although the rate of official migration has been further accelerating than otherwise,[16] recent developments in the international market for oil may affect the demand for foreign labour from the Arab oil countries. A recent study,[17] estimated that labour demand from the Arab oil-exporting countries would continue to increase at about 4 per cent per annum until 1985, and at a slightly slower rate thereafter. However, this was an extrapolation from previous trends, and did not take into account the recent slump in world oil prices or the cutbacks in the investment plans of some of the oil exporting countries. While Sudanese workers represent an insignificant proportion of total immigrant labour at present, the growing importance of "new" labour-exporters, such as South Korea and the

Philippines, may affect the Sudanese share of this market. Nevertheless, even if all these possiblities are taken into account, it is unlikely that the number of Sudanese working abroad will actually decline in the forseeable future. This is further accentuated by the fact that, given the stagnant economic conditions in the Sudan, the numbers wishing to leave will probably not go down.

There is a clear possibility that the changing pattern of demand for labour - with more emphasis on skilled and professional workers[18] - may lead to a decline in the number of unskilled workers departing. This is related to the fact that, more than absolute numbers, the problem is that of skilled workers departing.

There are, unfortunately, no exact estimates of the numbers of skilled or professional workers who have emigrated.[19] However, there is reason to believe that large numbers of such personnel are among the migrants. The survey of emigrants undertaken in Khartoum in August-September 1982 which also dealt only with official migration, but yielded more detailed information than is otherwise available, showed that only 37.5 per cent of the 216 migrants interviewed had no skills. The others all had either manual skills at present in short supply in urban Sudan (such as carpentry, electrical maintenance, driving etc.) or were trained to be professional or white collar workers.

(Tables A4 - A14 in the Appendix to Chapter 4 present most of the information obtained from this small survey. In what follows some summary information will be mentioned.)

The sample migrants showed much higher levels of literacy and education than an average cross-section of Sudanese population, even in urban areas. Only 12 per cent were illiterate, and most of these were refugees; while more than half of the sample were literate in at least two languages. Nearly 60 per cent had been educated up to secondary and higher levels. Although most of the sample migrants were young (71 per cent were in the age group 18-30 years) most of them had been employed for some years and had acquired work experience.[20] Only 16 per cent represented the export of open or disguised unemployment.

Over 90 per cent of the sample were males – mostly young and unmarried. Regionally, the central and eastern regions were significantly over-represented (nearly half of the sample) while the western regions were under-represented and there was no one at all from the south. To some extent this reflects the relative degrees of development of the various regions. Ten per cent of the sample were refugees, mainly from Eritrea, and they were predominantly illiterate women seeking employment as domestic servants in the Gulf countries. This also corresponds to the demand patterns in the host countries.

Saudi Arabia was the overwhelmingly favoured country of destination for the Sudanese migrants – over 77 per cent of the sample migrants were going there. This is confirmed by official recorded migration statistics (58 per cent of those officially working abroad in 1981 were in Saudi Arabia)[21] and by other estimates.[22] This reflects not only the close cultural and religious links between the two countries, but also geographical proximity and ease of entry. The annual hajj pilgrimage and omra journeys provide relatively easy methods of entering the country; also, visas and work permits for Sudanese are among the easiest to obtain for Saudi Arabia in relation to other countries. Kuwait and the other Gulf countries have recently started restricting the entry of Sudanese workers to some extent. Official migration to Libya was banned recently because of the strained political relations between the two countries, although presumably there are still many who simply cross the desert from North-west Sudan into Libya.

Besides this, Saudi Arabia is an Arab country with relative homogeneity of language and culture with the Sudanese North. The very influx of Sudanese workers has a cumulative causative impact, in that it creates in the host country a nexus of family and friends that potential migrants can utilise to facilitate their own entry.

Furthermore, the high salaries available in general in Saudi Arabia are combined with the religious incentives of being "in a holy place" for many Muslims.   The situation was aptly summed up by one migrant who chose to migrate to Saudi Arabia "to get the benefits of this life and the next".   This mixture of promised increases in material and spiritual welfare is apparently attractive to many Sudanese migrants.

In the sample, nearly 80 per cent of the migrants had arranged employment __before__ emigrating.   This very high percentage could be related to the fact that labour demand in host countries is no longer so high as to warrant migrants arriving in the country and then seeking employment.   However, the survey covered official migrants only, and it could well be that the majority of unofficial migrants actually do not arrange employment before departure.   For those with pre-arranged employment, contractors were the most significant agency for job offers - 38 per cent used this medium.   Personal contacts (family or friends) appear to be next in order of importance.

It was pointed out earlier that both demand and supply conditions in the Arab labour market are such that it would be difficult to stem the movement of labour from Sudan to the Arab oil-exporting countries.   In particular, given the stagnant domestic economy it is unlikely that domestic rates of remuneration for work will ever by high enough to be any incentive for Sudanese workers to stay on.   At present, the rates of pay in the host countries are around 6-10 times the pay for equivalent work in the Sudan.   Appendix Table A13 shows the differential between the wages presently received in Sudan by some sample migrants, and the prospective wages.   The data refer to Saudi Arabia alone, for selected migrants.[23]   The wage differential is very wide for most occupations - often being as much as 10 times, and in one case (that of a clerk) nearly 16 times, the existing salary in Sudan.   The implications of this are disturbing, as it is difficult to see how employers in Sudan can possibly compete with the much higher rates of remuneration available elsewhere.[24]

The immediate effect such large-scale emigration has on the labour markets in urban Sudan is that of creating shortages of

to the labour force within the Sudanese economy.   The official Labour
Department list of Sudanese working abroad in 1981 totalled
330,260.[14]   However, it is widely accepted that official emigration
forms only a minor proportion of the total number of emigrant
labourers.   Galal El Din's (1978) study estimated that unrecorded
migration could account for as much as 70-80 per cent of actual
migration for work from the Sudan.[15]   This means that the real
number of Sudanese workers abroad could be between 1.1 to 1.6
million.   Even if a more conservative estimate of an unofficial
migration rate of two-thirds is taken, this still implies a total of
one million Sudanese migrants for work abroad.

These numbers must be seen in relation to a total population of
approximately 18 million, a labour force of around 5.58 million, and
an urban workforce of little more than one million.   Thus the number
of Sudanese working abroad may even exceed the total urban labour
force of the country.   Even through all the migrants are not urban in
origin, in all probability most of them would have resided in a city
for at least some time before their departure from the Sudan.   In any
event they still represent a substantial withdrawal from the potential
urban labour force.

There is a possibility that the number of those leaving to work
abroad may taper off in the near future.   Although the rate of
official migration has been further accelerating than otherwise,[16]
recent developments in the international market for oil may affect the
demand for foreign labour from the Arab oil countries.   A recent
study,[17] estimated that labour demand from the Arab oil-exporting
countries would continue to increase at about 4 per cent per annum
until 1985, and at a slightly slower rate thereafter.   However, this
was an extrapolation from previous trends, and did not take into
account the recent slump in world oil prices or the cutbacks in the
investment plans of some of the oil exporting countries.   While
Sudanese workers represent an insignificant proportion of total
immigrant labour at present, the growing importance of "new"
labour-exporters,   such   as   South   Korea   and   the

spiralling real estate prices in the major urban centres of Sudan, especially in the period since the late 1970s. In some ways the issue becomes a circular one: people migrate for work in order to earn enough money to buy or build a house in a Sudanese city. However, since many people are doing the same thing, this pushes up the prices of houses and real estate. This in turn has two effects: firstly, it becomes necessary to stay away longer in the host country in order to earn the required (continuously growing) amount; secondly, it becomes very difficult for an urban Sudanese to buy or build a house without earning the type of high salary that is offered in Saudi Arabia, Libya or the Gulf countries. Thus the phenomenon of emigration (which, as is clear, is inextricably linked to the behaviour of the domestic economy) creates its own momentum. This makes it difficult to think of policies to control or channel migration, without an overall consistent macro-economic strategy.

money earned spent on consumps. R. would have invest.

Only 8 per cent of the migrants mentioned future avenues of expenditure that could be classed as productive investment. This very low percentage is not unexpected: it tends to be the norm in most poor countries experiencing labour emigration. Nevertheless, the implications for the domestic economy are ominous to say the least. Clearly, given the prevailing economic conditions in Sudan, very little of the money earned by labour abroad will be utilised to increase the productive potential of the country.

IV. Markets for skilled labour

The most immediately obvious feature of urban skilled labour markets in Sudan is that of major and growing shortages. This is related in a direct way to the emigration of labour discussed in the previous section; however, this is not the sole cause. The system of education and training also has a major role to play in this.

Although the exact extent of scarcity of skills is difficult to quantify because of the lack of data, there are certain occupations where domestic shortages are particularly acute and obvious. For

causes of skilled labour shortage
- emigration

shortage (1)

organised industry, there is a lack of <u>engineers</u>, <u>accountants</u> and <u>technicians</u>.　In all areas there is a growing shortage of <u>teachers</u> (2) (due primarily to emigration, since training facilites for teachers are adequate), which in turn has implications for producing qualified personnel in the future.　Other major shortages are of <u>mechanics</u>,

_R._　<u>electricians, plumbers, welders, carpenters and artisans generally</u>. The market for drivers (of cars as well as other transport vehicles such as trucks and buses) is increasingly reaching a situation of supply shortage.　Book-keepers and typists are other occupations for which it is difficult to find appropriately skilled people.　These shortages are not confined to the formal organised sector, but also extend to small-scale industries and the informal sector.

projected short

　　　The Government of the Sudan made an estimate of the expected shortages in skilled and professional manpower during the period of the 6 year Plan.　This is reproduced in Table A16 and shows that between 1978 and 1983 development projects and other activities were <u>expected to face a shortage of over 23,000 such people</u>.　But even this must be considered a gross underestimate, as it was made before the great increase in numbers of skilled workers emigrating, and does not include the impact of such movement.

　　　The structure of education and other training has much to answer for as regards these shortages.　It was pointed out earlier that Government recruitment policies, among other things, had operated to make liberal arts educations much more attractive in terms of job prospects than technical training.　In spite of recent efforts to alter it, the higher level education system remained heavily biased in favour of producing arts graduates with no particular technical skills.　<u>Furthermore, the preference for university education rather</u> <u>than vocational training, is still widespread</u>, so that the <u>universities continue to produce relatively large number of graduates</u>, while crucial and necessary <u>technical skills are not</u> developed. Table A15 shows the graduates of the various universities for the two years 1977/78 and 1978/79.　Nearly two-thirds of the 8,138 graduates had studied arts, social sciences, education or law, while a further

12 per cent had graduated in agriculture (a field where there are at present many unemployed graduates). The technical schools themselves tend to be academic rather than practical in orientation, so that employers prefer not to take on such graduates. This leads to the paradox that graduates of such schools find it difficult to find employment without prior experience, even while large numbers of technical posts remain unfilled for lack of suitable applicants. Those technical or vocational training institutes which do offer practical education are not sufficient in number, and do not have adequate facilities to meet the demand.[26]

For employers there are problems not only in hiring such labour, but also in keeping them. Firstly, it is increasingly difficult to find technically trained personnel with any experience at the stage of recruitment. This is common to all factories where technically trained personnel are required to control machinery.[27] The problem is that the chief competitor for such employers is not the domestic but the international demand for such skills, and, as was pointed out earlier, there is no way Sudanese employers can effectively compete. Thus the shortages, and consequent inability to hire suitable trained personnel, can affect the level of production.

Even more important for production, however, is the need for a stable workforce. This appears to be the gravest problem. Practically all the factories visited had problems of high turnover of skilled labour. Typically, skilled workers wait until they have acquired some experience in the factory and then depart.[28] In some factories the turnover of skilled labour is as high as 50 per cent per year,[29] and such labourers who leave their employment tend to do so to emigrate rather than to seek jobs elsewhere within Sudan. The only types of factories which do not appear to face such problems are either multinational subsidiaries operating in Sudan, which can afford to pay relatively higher wages, or those companies which require the type of skilled labour which is not in demand in the oil-exporting countries.[30]

Many employers, especially larger firms, are turning to offering incentives in terms of material benefits (such as an experience bonus) to persuade skilled labour to stay.   In some cases this has been successful, at least in restricting the numbers leaving.   In the majority of cases, however, this policy has had little or no impact, and implies merely an additional cost without any return.   A further cost is entailed when factories employ double the number of skilled workers required to run certain crucial machines or perform other important tasks that directly affect the level of production.[31] This serves as an insurance against the possible departure of such labour, but it does double the cost entailed.

One major effect of the present pattern of shortages is the relatively rapid diminution of wage differentials between non-manual and certain types of manual work.   Earlier it was shown how Government policy had resulted in relatively high rates of remuneration for white collar occupations in urban organised employment, especially when compared with manual work.   Recently, however, the shortages in particular manual skills (in particular technicians, mechanics, electricians, plumbers, carpenters and drivers - henceforth referred to as "skilled labour in short supply") have forced a shift away from this situation.   The increase in domestic demand for such skills has contributed to this process.   Table 4.1 presents the mean and mode values of wages (both annual and hourly) of the occupations graded according to skill, as found in the survey.

Some features of this table deserve note.   Firstly, there is not much variation (especially as regards the mode values per annum) between the different types of occupation.   But more than this, the difference between the mean annual wages for skilled labour in short supply and white collar jobs is only 2 per cent.   (The difference is greater for mean wages per hour, which indicates that such skilled labour works longer hours per week, and perhaps more weeks per year, than white collar workers.)   This is remarkably little by the standards of most third-world economies, and even when compared to the wage structure in urban Sudan 10 years earlier.

This same pattern is shown in more detail in Table 4.2 which
presents some wage statistics for particular skilled and white collar
occupations.   Unlike Table 4.1, this table refers to workers in Sudan
only (excluding those Sudanese workers at present working abroad who
were covered by the survey).   The comparison between particular white
collar jobs (such as clerk) and skilled manual jobs shows that in
annual terms the latter may be better off.   Wages per hour tend to be
lower in most cases, except for particularly scarce skills such as
carpenters and technicians.   Drivers of cars show surprisingly high
rates of remuneration.

Table 4.1: Wages by skill of occupation(£S)

Type of occupation	Annual				Hourly	
	Mean	Mode	Max	Min	Mean	Mode
Unskilled	1,009	720	21,600	50	0.44	0.19
Semi-skilled	1,398	720	18,000	250	0.63	0.31
Skilled	1,659	1,200	24,000	200	0.79	0.36
Skilled in short supply	2,033	1,800	14,400	200	0.80	0.42
White collar	2,078	720	24,000	300	1.09	0.31
Professional	5,779	3,600	36,000	1,562	2.51	1.04

Notes to Table: (1)   This includes some migrants at present working
in oil-exporting countries, which account for
the high maximum values.

(2)   The low minimum values for all except the
professional groups refer to apprentices.

Source: Urban Labour Market Survey (1982).

Table 4.2: Mean and mode wages for some professional and skilled
occupational groups in Urban Sudan (£S)

Occupation	No. of observations	Annual		Hourly	
		Mean	Mode	Mean	Mode
Manager	19	6,600	3,600	2.97	0.70
Engineer	16	3,764	2,400	1.60	1.04
Accountant	6	6,401	2,136	2.94	0.99
Teacher	17	2,093	840	0.97	0.36
Clerk/book-keeper	58	1,349	840	0.60	0.52
Secretarial	11	1,428	1,296	0.63	0.56
Government	19	1,644	1,800	0.70	0.31
Technician	11	2,274	1,008	0.99	0.44
Mechanic	16	2,117	1,080	0.95	0.29
Carpenter	60	1,675	1,200	0.73	0.48
Blacksmith	118	1,378	1,200	0.62	0.21
Electrician	13	2,163	636	0.92	0.27
Plumber/welder	26	1,319	1,080	0.56	0.17
Driver (car)	44	2,115	1,800	0.80	0.44
Driver (rail, truck bus)	45	2,147	600	0.79	0.26
Tailor	37	1,339	720	0.50	0.22

Source: Urban Labour Market Survey (1982).

V. Markets for unskilled labour

Unskilled labour markets in urban Sudan have generally been assumed to be characterised by a relative surplus of labour.[32] This has been due to the slow growth of organised employment in the cities as well as the very high rate of rural-urban migration. Not that rates of open unemployment have been high - on the contrary they have been relatively low.[33] However, the overall belief has been that most urban areas in Sudan are characterised by high rates of disguised unemployment and under-employment.

There are many factors contributing to this general impression. Most of the substantial rural-urban migration is directed towards the three towns making up Greater Khartoum. This is as much a result of its geographical location as by virtue of its being the capital city and major industrial centre. Recently, with the improvement in transport links to Port Sudan, flows of labour into that city have increased substantially as well.

Push factors causing such migration into urban areas have been noted earlier. However, there are also some important pull factors. Wage or income differentials between the cities and the rural areas remain significant, especially as far as incomes from traditional peasant agriculture are concerned. Furthermore, emigration results in a pull to the cities, as potential emigrants from rural areas gather in urban centres as the preliminary step to making arrangements to work abroad. Emigration for work abroad (especially if it is done through official channels) involves delays, legalities, applications for passports, visas, etc. The Arab labour market is still fairly open for Sudanese; yet entry is obviously not as easy as to the domestic market, and there is no direct substitutability - so lags can be expected. Thus the ranks of potential emigrants from rural areas swell the numbers of unskilled labour in the cities, meanwhile getting absorbed into informal sector activities or seeking employment as casual labour in organised industry or services. Greater Khartoum and Port Sudan, being the major points of exit from Sudan, are particularly prone to this. Employers in both cities pointed out that at least some of their labour turnover involves migrants who essentially treated residence in the cities, and associated employment, as a stopgap arrangement.

Whatever the reasons, such migration implies pressure on the cities' infrastructure, essential services and living conditions generally. Real estate prices and house rents have gone up remarkably in the last few years (the former is probably more related to the inflow of remittances from abroad) and there is pressure on accommodation facilities. Transport has become a major problem, especially in Khartoum, while in Port Sudan a growing constraint is the shortage of potable water. Also, the growth in the number of migrants, in particular those who at first stay with kin or friends while searching for employment, implies an increase in the number of dependents who have to be supported out of given wages.

One feature that clearly would support the hypothesis of labour surplus in the unskilled labour markets is the behaviour of the real wage in recent years. Table A24 gives official statistics on weekly earnings in private sector establishments in the period 1973-79. Although such data must be viewed with caution[34] it does indicate broadly that real wages in the urban organised sector remained constant or increased slightly over the 1970s. This is consistent with the opinion of other writers on urban labour in Sudan.[35] However, since 1979 it is clear that urban real wages in the aggregate have declined. This is partly related to the very high rates of inflation: the official cost of living index (which is probably an underestimate - see table A27) for lower-salaried urban Sudanese went up from 412 in 1979 to more than 640 in 1981 - an increase of over 55 per cent.[36] Money wages have not kept pace with this increase. Nominal wages in the public sector have not increased by more than 12 per cent (through dearness allowances and other such subsidies).

Table 4.3 shows the behaviour in recent years of money wage rates for unskilled labour in some industries in the Khartoum area. In 5 out of 13 cases the basic money wage has not increased at all since 1979. In those cases where there has been an increase (usually in the form of an abrupt jump in one year, related to a new collective agreement) the change has not been sufficient to keep pace with the price rise. Thus, in most of the cases of increasing money wages portrayed in Table 4.3, wages have gone up by around 40 per cent between 1979 and 1982. Enquiries in factories visited during the survey revealed that money wages in major private sector establishments, when they have gone up, have increased by 20-30 per cent on average. This, combined with the information in Table 4.3 and the behaviour of the cost-of-living index, implies that there has been a definite decline in the real wages of unskilled urban labour, often in the region of 25-30 per cent.

The fall in real wages in many sectors of the unskilled labour market has resulted in wage levels which are very unrealistic. In September 1982, in the public sector the lowest wage grades range from £S28 to £S50 per month. Given the prevailing price levels of essential commodities in both Khartoum (as shown in Table A27) and Port Sudan, this wage is not adequate to support a worker alone, much less his/her family.

This decline would be compatible with the idea of labour surplus in the unskilled sector. However, there are other features which indicate that the labour surplus may be more apparent than real. Many employers, especially in Khartoum North and Salabona (the industrial areas of the two cities) complained of difficulties in hiring and keeping unskilled labourers. Furthermore, the very high rates of labour emigration, especially in relation to the total urban workforce, would suggest that there are tendencies towards labour shortage even in the unskilled sector, That this expresses itself not in absolute shortages but in high turnover rates and related phenomena may be due to the industrial stagnation and the possible rigidity of investment in responding to changing economic conditions.

Table 4.3: Trends in money wage rates for unskilled workers 1975-1982
            (selected companies in Khartoum)

£S per month	1975	1978	1979	1980	1981	1982
Small (< 100 workers)						
Cotton cord and wax	28	35	35	35	35	35
International perfumery	n.a.	35-40	40	40	40	45
Umdurman cloth factory	n.a.	28	28	28	28	28
Sudanese cosmetics	n.a.	n.a.	n.a.	45	45	45
Yamstein soap factory	16.5	28	35	35	35	35
Medium (100< 300)						
Packing house	16.5	28	28	32	32	40
Nile paints works	16.5	16.5	40	40	40	40
Sponge and plastic shoes	16.5	28	28	35	35	35
Elmadeh oil mill	n.a.	21	25	45	50	60
Big (300< 1000)						
Karam biscuits	16.5	28	28	28	28	40
Hillal footwear	16.5	16.5	28	28	28	40
Large (> 1000)						
Bata shoes	n.a.	28-80	28-80	28-80	28-80	28-95
Sudan textiles	16.5	22	28	28	28	28

Source: Data collected from the Federation of Trade Unions, Khartoum.

Some crucial features of unskilled labour markets stand out at first glance: the very high rates of labour turnover in most private organised sector firms, the relation between organised and unorganised employment remuneration, the mobility of unskilled labour between formal and informal sectors, and the growth of secondary occupation. All of these phenomena are closely linked and in some ways causally related. While the first two features are substantiated by the survey, it is unfortunate that the survey data cannot highlight the latter two characteristics.[37]

High turnover is a pervasive problem in some industries. Some employers reported rates of turnover of nearly 100 per cent in half a year.[38] The worst hit appears to be the textile industry, where in the three major factories in operation at present, between 4 to 7 workers leave every day, and less than the total required number of workers is employed because they leave so rapidly.[39] The textile industry may be a special case because historically it has faced similar problems[40] and Sudanese labourers have never considered it an attractive employment.

In another sense, however, the situation of textiles may not be so special, in that it belongs to the category of "declining industries" as mentioned in the first chapter. In a general sense, manufacturing industry in Sudan is either stagnant or declining, and faces numerous problems of rising costs from sources other than unskilled labour. Thus it may be prepared to pay only a certain amount as wages for unskilled labour, and this has implied low and declining real wages.

From the point of view of labour, the conclusion appears almost inevitable that the rate of turnover is related to the remuneration for work.[41] Factories which pay higher wages do not have high turnover rates and are usually able to secure a stable workforce. The very low real wages which are offered to begin with by most employers are simply not sufficient for independent economic existence, and so workers tend to move from job to job or employer to

Refugees may resort to same.

employer in the hope of securing more income.   Since strikes are
banned and trade union activity severely limited, they may have no way
of expressing their dissatisfaction other than simply leaving the job.

It should be noted that this turnover is not related to
agricultural seasonality, and on the whole the phenomenon is not one
of peasants migrating to the towns for a few months then going back to
farm their land or work as agricultural labour.   It is thus a
different phenomenon from the historically observed seasonal migration
pattern.   Nor did employers appear to face any seasonal variations in
difficulty of hiring labour.   Rather, this turnover seems to be a
form of "urban nomadism" with workers going from employer to employer
within the urban area as part of of their survival strategies.   The
other main labour market with which this turnover interacts is the
international one - it could be possible to link some of the turnover
with labour emigration.

urban nomad-

Along with high turnover rates, absenteeism is a major problem.
In most of the factories visited, the absenteeism rate fluctuated
between 15-30 per cent daily and sometimes even 40 per cent daily.
Some employers (especially in Port Sudan) try to circumvent this
problem on a casual, daily basis, but this is not possible for many
employers.   Such dramatically high rates of labour turnover and
absenteeism have obvious implications for productivity and costs in
enterprises, and add to the other constraints on industrial production.

R.

why low wage in many?

Given the disadvantages of such high labour turnover, why do employers
accept this situation when the remedy (higher wages for unskilled
labour) appears to be within their reach?   One possibility is that,
given the general stagnation in the manufacturing sector, and the
decline in particular industries, as well as the high costs that have
to be met for other inputs, employers in these areas are not really in
a position to pay higher wages.[42]   Furthermore, for some employers
at least, the trade-off between high labour turnover and low real
wages may not warrant an increase in wages.   That is, the positive
effects of a low real wage rate may outweigh the negative

Q

since there is excess supply of unskilled labour employers may prefer high labour turnover to paying higher wages effects of high labour turnover. Also turnover prevents the consolidation of labour and growth of workers' organisations. This may be seen as a positive benefit. Although strikes are banned, there are cases of entrenched trade unions and powerful workers' groups posing real threats to employers - the railway workers of Atbara and the dockworkers of Port Sudan are obvious examples.

The high rates of absenteeism described for the organised private sector (and the even higher rates observable in public enterprises and Government offices) may be related to another feature: that of the the growing reliance of many urban workers on subsidiary occupations to supplement their incomes. Most often these occupations are informal sector activities, and may range from money exchange to petty trading, porterage or carting in the marketplace, etc.[43] Thus the distinction between formal and informal sectors becomes even more fluid, as labour moves from one to the other and may simultaneously have occupations in both.

Although the growth of such activities cannot be quantified, definite indications (which corroborate interviews and observations made during the survey) are given by the high rates of absenteeism and also by the rates of remuneration of such occupations compared to organised sector employment. Table 4.4 presents some wage statistics for various unskilled jobs. Production workers and spinners, etc. who typically work in organised sector establishments, do not receive wages substantially higher than those engaged in casual "market-place" jobs. Thus, carwashers, shoe polishers, porters, cart-pullers and auctioneers, for example, may get very high incomes. The variation is quite high, but the simple possibility of very high returns should serve to attract people.

This is linked to the differential behaviour of the stagnating and prospering economic activities. In manufacturing and textiles, for example, workers get relatively low pay - particularly for spinning. On the other hand, bricklayers, who are involved in the booming construction industry, get relatively more. Likewise, services in general and petty trading are prospering, which explains the high remuneration in those areas.

The behaviour of the different sectors of the urban economy in response to the changing demand conditions implies also a change in the nature of urban wage determination. It has been suggested earlier that for the organised sector the wages in the government and public sector enterprises in some sense have acted as signals or wage-setters for other employers. The unorganised sector was seen to be more flexible and responsive to demand and supply conditions. However, as the "booming" urban sectors (services and petty trading) become important and such employers are able to offer higher rates of remuneration, they attract more labour, both skilled and unskilled, away from the public sector. The private organised sector now has to compete with these newly significant employers. The present time can be described as one of transition from the situation described earlier to one where the market demand forces are fundamental in the determination of wage levels and variations.

One of the areas where the difficulties caused by such a transition are most apparent is that of railway employment. Sudan Railways is the largest employer in the country. Run entirely by the public sector, it employs about 35,000-40,000 workers, approximately 27,000 of whom are based in the "railway city" of Atbara in the northern province. The wage rates prevailing in Sudan Railways, especially in the unskilled and semi-skilled groups, are as low as elsewhere in the public sector. The Urban Labour Market Survey (1982) found that the wages of unskilled production workers in the Railways varied between £S480-1,088 per annum, with a mode of £S684. More skilled occupations such as train drivers, fitters, machine operators and carpenters, received higher wages (fluctuating around £S1,200) which were still low when compared to their counterparts in the private sector. In very large urban centres such as Port Sudan and Khartoum, the possibilities open for diversification of income sources by engaging in sudsidiary jobs go some way towards rectifying

Table 4.4: Wage rates for selected unskilled occupations
in urban Sudan (Males only)

	£S Annual				Hourly	
Occupation	Mean	Mode	Max	Min	Mean	Mode
Production worker	1,045	720	4,584	280	0.56	0.31
Spinner	905	576	1,590	336	0.39	0.31
Bricklayer	1,310	1,000	3,840	288	0.56	0.36
Tanner	1,100	864	1,440	864	0.52	0.38
Own Trade	3,038	1,440	18,000	400	1.16	0.38
Waiter	626	540	800	540	0.23	0.14
Messenger	1,074	480	2,700	480	0.39	0.21
Guard	796	840	2,196	360	0.32	0.14
Car washer	1,343	1,440	3,600	500	0.45	0.13
Shoe polisher	1,439	400	2,920	400	0.48	0.14
Porter	1,260	1,080	2,160	1,080	0.43	0.29
Salesman	819	1,000	1,200	360	0.32	0.42
Cart puller	1,855	2,160	3,150	250	0.69	0.11
Auctioneer	2,520	1,440	3,600	1,440	0.67	0.38
Laundry	2,145	2,130	2,160	2,130	0.57	0.57
Own café	5,800	7,200	7,200	3,000	1.57	0.80
Gardener	642	336	792	336	0.32	0.24

Source: Urban Labour Market Survey (1982)

this imbalance.   But such options are not always open in
cities - thus Atbara, which is based almost entirely on the popula.
employed by the Railways, is not an urban economy suffuciently larg\
or diversified as to offer many alternative sources of secondary
income.   This implies that wages from the primary occupation are, per
force, the mainstay income of the workers' households.   Given the
unrealistically low level of real wages, it may not be altogether
surprising that one of the main instances of organised trade union
protest in the recent past has been the railway workers' strike of
1981, based primarily in Atbara.   The railway workers historically
have been among the more militant sections of the working class in
Sudan; nevertheless, it is probable that economic grievances over
wages were exacerbated by the absence of alternative employment
opportunities.   Thus, it is clear that developments in the urban
labour markets may prove to be useful in explaining the presence or
absence of politcal tension in urban Sudan.

VI.   Specific features of urban labour markets

This section discusses some aspects of urban labour markets in
the Sudan, specifically in relation to various forms of market
segmentation.   The possibilities of labour market segmentation by
industry (resulting from differential growth prospects and demand
conditions) and sector has already been considered.   Here, other
forces making for segmentation - such as sex, region and type of
employer - are dealt with.   The analysis refers to both skilled and
unskilled groups.

Firstly, some characteristics of the sample households should be
mentioned.   Because the sample was not random but purposive, it does
not provide a representative cross-section of the urban population.
Thus the wages and income data do not represent average urban earnings
(especially since a greater proportion of skilled workers in general
was interviewed, in an effort to identify as many types of workers as
possible).   With these caveats in mind, Table A26 shows some income
data relating to the sample households.   It is apparent that more

than half of the sample households showed a per capita income of under £S400 a year. Even when calculated in terms of adult equivalent, 48 per cent (or nearly half) had under £S400 a year per adult equivalent. This amounts to a monthly income per adult of £S16.67 - clearly very low when compared with prevailing price levels for essential foodstuffs and other items of mass consumption, in the urban areas. Table A27 gives some indication of the level of market prices in Khartoum in July 1982, a month before the survey was undertaken.[44]

The size of the households in the sample varied from 1 to 18 and the average size of all sample households was 5.67. Table A17 gives the distribution of households by wage brackets (by wage of household head and by average wage in household) as well as other information such as average household size and dependent-earner ratio. It appears that the latter two variables do not show any systematic variation with wage brackets.

According to Labour Laws in the Sudan, women should be given equal pay for equal work. However, the survey data show fairly consistent differentials between the pay received by men and women in similar occupations. Table 4.1 presents wage differentials between sexes for selected occupations. In every one of the cases (except for that of secretary/typist) female workers receive lower remuneration than male workers in terms of mean and mode payments. This implies that women are usally concentrated in the lower pay scales. This discrepancy holds even when the data are analysed by hour, indicating that for such occupations men do not work any longer hours than women.[45]

This is confirmed by Table A19 which presents wage brackets by sex for the main occupational groups. Firstly, there are hardly any female skilled workers in the sample. This may reflect a sampling bias, but it also is related to the fact that in urban Sudan many jobs are sex specific. For example, women do not indulge in the construction activity[46] or in most forms of skilled manual

Table 4.5: Wage differentials between sexes for selected occupations in Sudan

| | £S | | | | | |
| Occupation | Annual | | | | Hourly | |
	Mean	Mode	Max	Min	Mean	Mode
Medical						
Male	2,709	2,580	8,400	600	4.12	1.17
Female	1,560	600	3,000	600	0.83	0.50
Teacher						
Male	2,093	840	8,400	720	0.97	0.36
Female	740	720	840	616	0.37	0.31
Government						
Male	1,644	1,800	4,800	660	0.70	0.31
Female	1,144	720	1,500	720	0.51	0.31
Secretary						
Male	1,428	1,296	1,560	1,296	0.63	0.56
Female	1,768	720	3,936	720	0.78	0.31
Clerk						
Male	1,349	840	6,000	480	0.60	0.52
Female	837	630	1,080	630	0.38	0.30
Salesman						
Male	819	1,000	1,200	360	0.32	0.42
Female	250	200	300	200	0.12	0.12
Tailor						
Male	1,339	720	3,600	300	0.50	0.22
Female	1,040	360	3,600	300	0.41	0.16
Spinner						
Male	906	576	1,590	336	0.39	0.31
Female	637	611	888	456	0.27	0.26
Production Worker						
Male	1,045	720	4,584	280	0.56	0.31
Female	768	576	2,016	280	0.39	0.24

labour.   Secondly, within groups female workers are concentrated in
the lower wage brackets to a far greater extent than male workers.
In white collar occupations they are generally engaged in secretarial
or clerical task, while in unskilled work they are more likely to be
found in assembly line jobs or activities such as spinning.

The distribution of workers by region presents some interesting
features.   As was pointed out earlier, most of the urban workers in
the main cities are migrants from rural areas.   Many of them come
from the western and southern regions of Sudan.   Table A20 gives the
distribution of workers by wage brackets and main occupational groups,
according to region of origin.   Most of the workers appear to come
from the central region (the provinces of Khartoum, Blue Nile, White
Nile and Gezira), and the central and northern region workers would
seem to have a higher proportion of workers in the   £S1,000 group
than others.[47]   Workers from the south and west fare relatively
well in relation to other groups in the professional and white collar
occupations and average in the category of unskilled workers.
However, in the skilled worker group, they appear to have a lower
proportion in the higher wage group than the other regions.   This by
itself should not lead to any inferences, however, since the
differences may be due to degree of skill and scarcity of the
particular occupation, etc.   Table A29 gives additional data on this.

It is generally accepted that urban wages in Sudan vary with the
type of employer.   This view is definitely confirmed by data from
this survey, but not according to the pattern which is usually
supposed.   For example, it was generally thought that the public
sector paid higher wages than the private sector[48] and that wages in
the organised sector varied positively with the size of industrial
establishment.[49]   However, neither of these is really the case.
For all categories of workers (professional and white collar, skilled
and unskilled) private employment in general seems to offer better
remuneration.   Table 4.6 below shows that the mean and maximum wages
per year for all categories of workers are higher in the private
sector   than   in   the   public.   This   reflects   the

Table 4.6: <u>Wage rates by type of employer</u> (£S per year)

Type of occupation	Public	Private
Professional		
Mean	1,608	4,855
Max.	4,800	36,000
Min.	336	900
White Collar		
Mean	1,193	2,470
Max.	3,600	24,000
Min.	480	300
Skilled		
Mean	1,448	1,848
Max.	7,200	14,400
Min.	240	200
Unskilled production		
Mean	923	1,105
Max.	2,160	4,800
Min.	336	280
Unskilled service		
Mean	762	1,195
Max.	1,800	7,200
Min.	360	200

<u>Source</u>: Urban Labour Market Survey (1982).

change in the pattern of wage determination discussed in the previous section.   Tables A22 (A,B,C) give a more detailed breakdown of wages by type of employer.[50]   Self-employed workers seem to be in the most advantageous position (especially in the skilled occupations).   The public sector and the Government appear to be the employers with the greatest concentration of workers in the lower wage groups.   In a sense this fits the pattern found in urban areas of other less developed economies, where the security and lower remuneration of public sector employment can be contrasted with the greatest insecurity and high potential remuneration of private (especially self-) employment.

Table A25, which deals specifically with wage variations in organised employment (both public and private) according to the size of the industrial establishment, does not really confirm the hypothesis of wages varying positively with size.   The data refer to skilled and production workers only, and do not show any systematic pattern.   (If only the groups "small" and "large" are taken, then the data would support the above hypothesis.   This may account for its widespread prevalence.)   The existing belief may be due to the existence of some large "model employers" (usually multinational subsidiaries using relatively capital-intensive techniques) who upset the averages.   Table 4.7 below also suggests that urban organised wages are not correlated with the size of the employing establishment.

VII.   Refugees and urban labour markets in the Sudan

The somewhat complex picture of urban labour markets in the Sudan takes on a special significance when the problems of, and possibilities for absorption of, refugees are considered.   It is increasingly being recognised by refugee host countries that no medium term solution to improving the condition of refugees can exclude possibilities for income-generating activities by the refugees.   In the case of the Sudan, in urban areas this would involve entry into, and absorption by, the various labour markets.

Entry & absorption

Table 4.7: Wage rates by size of firm (£S per year)

Occupation type	Very small 50	Small 50 100	Medium 100 300	Big 300 1,000	Large 1,000 5,000	Very large 5,000
Professional						
Mean	4,200	1,818	5,593	4,309	2,250	2,839
Max.	--	3,060	10,666	36,000	3,000	6,000
Min.	--	1,212	1,562	616	1,500	720
White Collar						
Mean	806	1,667	3,208	1,812	1,320	2,257
Max.	840	6,000	11,200	6,840	--	24,000
Min.	772	720	900	630	--	300
Skilled						
Mean	1,488	1,520	2,214	2,000	1,908	1,334
Max.	2,820	14,400	6,516	12,000	3,060	4,440
Min.	720	216	810	300	840	200
Unskilled production						
Mean	550	859	1,822	938	1,080	910
Max.	1,080	1,800	4,584	4,800	1,521	3,600
Min.	280	348	585	288	720	336
Unskilled service						
Mean	1,476	683	1,717	687	860	787
Max.	3,600	1,200	2,700	1,440	1,068	1,800
Min.	420	336	780	360	768	364

Source: Urban labour market survey (1982).

It was remarked earlier that the data from this survey (in particular Table A20) indicate that those refugees who are employed seem to be doing relatively well in terms of remuneration, even in relation to other Sudanese groups. However, such data cannot be used to form conclusions about the status of refugees for some very important reasons. Firstly, the sample of refugees was very small, and furthermore there are possibilities that it may have been biased, in that the relatively better off refugees may have been chosen.

A better idea of the relative position of refugees can be had from looking at particular occupations. One of the most common male refugee occuptions within the Sudan is that of truck-driving. A sample of 9 refugee[51] and 6 Sudanese truck-drivers reveals that the refugees receive approximately 25 per cent less than the Sudanese.[52] The mean for refugees is £S2,633 per annum while that for Sudanese is £S3,290 per annum. Furthermore, the difference in wages calculated by hour is even greater - Sudanese truck-drivers earn 62.5 per cent more than refugee truck-drivers in this sample (mainly because the latter work longer hours per week).

However, this does not necessarily reflect greater exploitation of refugee truck-drivers, as the situation is more complex. Many of the refugees are employed either by other refugees who own the company or by a co-operative, and in either case some of the profits may apparently be used for donation or subsidy to particular refugee political organisations.[53] Thus the lower wages accepted by refugees in this case may reflect a voluntary choice on their part.

As for other occupations, the refugees in the sample receive equivalent or slightly better rates of pay than Sudanese.[54] It appears that those refugees who are able to find employment are not much worse off than the local population. Refugee workers also tend to be concentrated in particular occupations and sector - for e.g. services in general, and hotels and restaurants in particular as cooks and waiters.

MB - This is wrong now because of the changes in regard to work permits & Kasha.

Granted that refugees in employment do not face particular problems, it is still difficult for refugees to find work. The main constraints to obtaining employment for refugees are at present merely legal. Thus, refugees have to possess work permits and identity certificates to obtain employment in the organised sector. If they wish to set up their own enterprise or business they require business permits. These should not be difficult to get, but in practice there are many delays and often rejections of applications by lower-level bureaucracy. This is essentially a problem of administrative lack of control, because official policy statements (and the views of the higher echelons of the Government) insist that refugees should not face any problem in acquiring such permits.

Given the situation described earlier in the various labour markets in the urban areas, there appear to be many possibilities for refugees. There are major and severe shortages of particular types of skilled labour, and if refugees could be trained to fill these gaps it would be equivalent to (and less expensive for the country than) any programme of replacement migration. Unfortunately, there is a tendency for skilled and trained refugees to emigrate as well, and - considering the incentives already described for Sudanese to emigrate to work abroad - there appears little chance that this tendency will diminish in the near future.

There are particular areas where it appears that all that is required are better channels of information, and perhaps a sort of labour office for refugees.[55] For example, in Port Sudan many employers pointed out that they had difficulty in recruiting labour because of a requirement of good working knowledge of English. This is the case in many factories using European technology where the on-the-job training to man the machines must be, or is preferably, carried out in English.[56] It is frequently mentioned that Ethiopian/Eritrean refugees from urban areas tend to have a better working knowledge of English than urban Sudanese youth.

[Handwritten margin note, left side, top]: constraints!

[Handwritten margin note, left]: NB

[Handwritten margin note, left]: Why do R. emigrate?

[Handwritten margin note, bottom]:

NB The problem in the Sudan is not absence of legal privileges but rather lack of uniform policy and practice. The lower-level bureaucracy does not know or deliberately ignores regulations or laws that relate to rights of R.S. Lack of administrative control.

shortages

The skill survey carried out in refugee camps in 1982,[57] found the presence of many skilled workers in the refugee settlements. These included those skills at present scarce in the urban areas, such as mechanics, electricians, carpenters, drivers and typists. A substantial percentage of these skilled groups were found at present to be either unemployed (10-23 per cent) or working as farmers/farm labourers (8-26 per cent). Lack of use of such skills not only implies the possible loss of these skills, but also waste of potentially valuable inputs to the urban labour markets. Given the nature of the markets for skilled labour as discussed in section IV, the addition of such skills could only benefit the overall functioning of the urban economies.

VIII. Government intervention in urban labour markets

Even if the Government of the Sudan did not actively intervene in urban labour markets through labour legislation, wage policies, etc., it would still play a major role in affecting wage structure and employment patterns. The Government itself employs a large number of people within the bureaucracy, as well as teachers and staff in the five major universities and other institutes, and in schools throughout the country. Another major source of urban employment is Sudan Railways, controlled by the Government. Furthermore, public enterprises employ another large segment of the urban workforce.[58] Thus altogether a significant proportion of the urban labour force (even if not the majority) is affected by the Government's employment policy.[59]

The effects of the pattern of recruitment and wage structure within the Government and public sector have already been discussed. It is clear that past policies of the Government to a large extent have been responsible for an imbalance between the educational structure and youth priorities for employment, on the one hand, and vocational and manpower needs of the economy on the other.

However, besides this role of employer, the Government also intervenes in urban labour markets through minimum wage legislation, bills in industrial and labour relations and the functioning of Labour Offices in the major urban centres. The question is really to what extent such intervention is successful in achieving its aims, and whether it could be modified beneficially in any way.

The Government started to enforce a legal minimum wage in 1974 (before that the public sector minimum was supposed to act as a "guideline" for the private sector). However, the minimum wage policy has several important defects. Firstly, it does not cover the majority of workers, but only permanent workers in the organised sector. This eliminates all those working as casual labour, or for very small workshops or private individuals - that is, the majority of the urban labour force. In fact the latter group is largely unprotected by any labour legislation. (This is true for even such supposedly essential aspects as accident insurance for illnesses/injury contracted on the job in the case of physically dangerous tasks.) Therefore, even if the minimum wage were effective, it would only cover a minority of urban workers. Secondly, the minimum wage contains no element of inflation indexation; thus, given the rapid rates of price rise in urban Sudan, it speedily tends to become outdated. This leads to the situation described in Section V, where the low nominal wages are simply not adequate to meet the consumption needs of an urban family, and consequently other sources of income are sought. *Why R. do not work*

The Labour Offices themselves have a large number of functions to fulfil in the major urban centres. The Labour Offices are responsible for the implementation of the 11 Labour Laws; a significant proportion of hiring in is done through their mediation; they are meant to arbitrate in industrial disputes and resolve cases of dispute between workers and employers; they are responsible for the issue of identity cards and work permits. Given the large number of tasks assigned to it, it is unfortunate that the staff and facilities of the Labour Offices[60] are not always adequate to meet all these tasks. This results in delays, inefficiencies and associated problems.   It is necessary to streamline at least some of the functioning of the Labour Offices, or to limit some of their tasks, if they are to be more effective in the roles they play.

Some of the policy proposals that emerge from the above discussion are:

(1)   More urban workers should be brought under the purview of wage and industrial legislation.   At present only a section of the workforce in organised industry is covered by labour laws.   Casual workers, both in large companies and in small workshops, as well as those employed by private individuals, do not have any of the forms of protection by legislation (such as injury insurance, etc., which are often considered to be fundamental) open to the "privileged" workers.   It is possible to extend the purview of acts such as the Industrial Relations Bill of 1981 to cover more urban workers.   However, this would involve more costs of enforcement and extend the duties and responsibilities of the labour offices.

(2)   Minimum wage legislation has a very limited impact, primarily on the organised workforce.   However, it is not index-linked to inflation at all, and therefore it speedily becomes out of date, especially given the high rates of inflation in the country.   To be at all effective, some form of index linking of the minimum wage would be necessary.

(3)   As pointed out earlier, the labour offices are in need of some reconstitution.   Some of their duties could be simplified by streamlining the procedures for obtaining identity cards and work permits.   (At present these are very complicated.)   Furthermore, there should be more training of labour officers in the analysis of employment conditions in various sectors of the labour market, not just the organised sector workforce.

(4)   Because of the nature of government involvement in urban labour markets, the Labour Offices are potentially significant as data banks on urban labour. Unfortunately, although large quantities of information are passed on to the Labour Offices every day, there is no organised procedure for the collection, classifiction and analysis of such data. More officers should be trained in collecting data for research purposes with a view to facilitating a better understanding of the nature of the workforce and conditions of employment.

IX. Concluding remarks

The earlier sections have described some of the dynamic processes at work in the economy as well as some of the main features of urban labour markets. The picture that emerges is a very complex one, replete with phenomena that may appear contradictory at first glance. One way of trying to reconcile these various forces and to see if they conform to any more systematic pattern, is to hypothesise about the impact of the processes that have been mentioned.

What follows is an attempt to synthesise the various aspects of urban labour markets. This is put forward not as a definitive explanation of all the features, but as a suggestion towards a deeper understanding of them. Although the starting point is the empirical reality described in the earlier sections, the speculations that follow are not necessarily susceptible to empirical verification, given the paucity of data.

We are concerned with a less developed economy with low population density, a very low level of industrialisation, and heavy reliance on the export of one primary crop - cotton. Per capita income is extremely low (even in relation to other less developed countries) but the inequality of income distribution is less extreme than in other similar economies. There has been an attempt by the Government to increase productivity in agriculture and develop the industrial base through a programme of public investment and encouragement of private investment. In agriculture this was attempted through expanison of mechanised farmland and development of more irrigated schemes and rehabilitation of existing ones. In industry, attempts are made to develop the textile industry, food and beverage processing, and also some heavy industries such as cement and machine tools.

Unfortunately, such investments come up against a resource constraint in general and a foreign exchange constraint in particular. The latter is affected by a coincidence of domestic and international forces: the production of raw cotton declines, the world market for cotton slumps and prices fall correspondingly, and a sudden and massive increase in world oil prices causes a significant increase in this country's import bill.

This leads to large, continuous and growing balance of payments deficits, and consequent curtailment of the investment programme. The foreign exchange crisis affects industry by creating shortages of imported machinery and raw materials, and by reducing the availability of one of the most crucial inputs for production and transport - fuel. Thus employment in urban organised industry tends to stagnate.

Meanwhile, the agricultural situation has also deteriorated, because of a decline in productivity in the irrigated cotton producing schemes, stagnation of traditional peasant farming, and growing difficulties of nomadic pastoralism. The slight increase in rural employment through the extension of mechanised farming is not enough to make up for the decline in the other agricultural sectors. This creates a growing tendency for a rural push of population into the cities in search of employment and income.

The growing pressure of population in the main cities, in a context of stagnating organised employment, creates obvious difficulties. However, at this stage another factor intervenes: the emergence of a vast demand for labour, both skilled and unskilled, in the oil-exporting countries of the Middle East. The development of this market results in a major and increasing flow of migrants from the Sudan, who are attracted by the vastly superior salaries being offered in the labour-importing countries.

The departure of increasing numbers of skilled labourers adds to the difficulties of industrial production and development of social infrastructure. The shortages caused by skilled labour emigration compound the problems caused by imbalances in the educational system. Within the urban areas, this also affects markets for unskilled labour: firstly by causing increased production costs and shortfalls which adversely affect industrial employment in general; secondly by allowing for some upward mobility of unskilled labour through the sheer necessity of filling in gaps; and finally, indirectly through remittances.

Although large numbers of skilled personnel depart, the greater proportion of migrants is relatively unskilled. Migration of unskilled labour helps to increase the fluidity of urban labour in general, it increases labour turnover, and it (indirectly) affects the urban sectors of informal employment.

All migration results in remittances, even if these do not correspond to expected levels. The inflow of remittances is not significant enough to alleviate substantially the country's foreign exchange crisis. However, it does cause important domestic changes. On the one hand it implies an increase in effective demand *NB* without any concomitant increase in production, thus leading to inflation. When remittances come in the form of goods (e.g. cars and consumer durables) they imply further foreign exchange expenditures as well. On the other hand, this increase in effective demand is not spread equally across sectors. Essentially it reflects a shift in income distribution and consequent changes in tastes. Incomes become more unequally distributed. Particular sectors face a declining pattern of demand, while others (mainly real estate and construction, transport, hotels and restaurants and other services) face a boom

NB - Impact of remittance.

situation. This in turn implies a shift in employment and investment patterns in the urban areas. Labour moves, especially through informal employment, to the boom areas. In the declining areas, there is some degree of investment rigidity, which is expressed in falling real wages and high turnover. Government and public sector employment and wage levels remain unchanged in nominal terms (which implies a decline in wages in real terms)[61] and labour employed within that sector increasingly seeks additional income from informal activities particularly in the booming sectors. This may be through the growing importance of subsidiary occupations for individuals, or the diversification of occupations and sources of income within households. The rapid rate of inflation and sectoral demand increase lead to the development and consolidation of a mercantile/ speculative group, which then provides an additional source of demand from within the economy. These may be joined by (or may be the same people as) prosperous agricultural landowners in the mechanised rain fed sector, where the concentration of land control has been increasing.

Thus the processes in the economy and in the various labour markets would appear to be affected by two major forces: emigration abroad and the pattern of investment   emigration creates a new structure of demand (through remittances) and affects the labour markets in ways described in Section III. The main policy instrument in the hands of the Government is investment. However, the nature of investment in recent years has been such as to acccentuate inequalities rather than rectify imbalances.

The above describes one possible scenario which helps to explain the particular patterns of labour exchange that were observed in the urban economy of Sudan. The nature of wage variation by occupation, the growth of secondary occupations, the high mobility of labour and the low productivity levels could all be explained with the terms of this scenario. However, this does not provide a definitive account of labour processes in the urban centres of Sudan, primarily because of the many gaps in our knowledge that still remain. The following suggestions for further research would go some way towards filling these gaps.

(1)   The nature of internal migration in Sudan needs to be understood more clearly.   In particular, the push factors in labour supply areas such as Darfur, Kordofan and the southern provinces should be analysed.   This would involve an analysis of the prevailing economic conditions in these areas (and particularly the trends in income and employment) as well as a survey on the nature of the migrants and the usual periods of migration for work, as well as their destinations.   One hypothesis that could be tested is that as agricultural schemes in the irrigated and rain fed areas demand less migrant labour from the west, such labour increasingly heads for the towns (especially Khartoum) and possibly abroad, in search of employment.

(2)   There has been some speculation in this paper on the change in the nature of urban wage determination in Sudan.   This requires further research.   Specifically it requires more precise indicators of the relations between labour demand and supply in the various sectors, as well as analysis of different forms of urban wage contracts.   A project to analyse this in detail could also look at forms of open and disguised unemployment in the urban areas, an aspect not covered by this chapter.

(3)   The effects of labour emigration abroad, in terms of creating shortages of skilled labour, should be studied.   Such shortages could be quantified to some degree, through information taken from major urban employers and a random sample of small employers.   Also the precise effects on production (and investment) of such shortages of particular skills, could be analysed.

(4)   Further research is necessary also for understanding the changing pattern of income distribution and demand.   This has important indirect effects on the labour markets, both urban and rural.

Footnotes

[1] 4.27 per cent increase per annum to Greater Khartoum in the period 1955/56 - 1973/74, and probably more since. MEFIT, Roma, quoted in A.S. Oberai (1975).

[2] ILO (1976) projections based on data from the 1973 Census of Sudan.

[3] The figures projected for 1982 are as follows:

(000s)

	Urban	All Sudan
Male	2,499	9,505
Female	2,198	9,247
Total	4,697	18,752

Source: Statistical Abstract of Sudan, 1981, p. 11.

[4] Projections based on the 1973 Census of Sudan, made by ILO (1976), Technical Paper No. 8. This estimate is based on a projected labour force participation rate of 31 per cent for 1980, and a share of urban labour in the total labour force of 16 per cent.

[5] Thus, an ILO study based on a survey in Khartoum in 1974, found that a substantial proportion of rural migrants into other cities viewed this first move as a step to the ultimate aim of arriving in Greater Khartoum. A.S. Oberai, (1975) op. cit.

[6] Table A1 in the Appendix gives the 1982 pay grades in the public sector corporations and in the Government.

[7] Table A15 in the Appendix shows the number of graduates (or students enrolled in the case of new universities) of the major institutes of higher education, by subject.

[8] Exceptions to this usually come either from textile factories or from very small establishments, at the lower end; and from very large capital-intensive multinational subsidiaries at the upper end.

[9] On the basis of a sample of 15 factories in Port Sudan and information given by the Port Sudan Labour Office.

[10] This is discussed in greater detail in section V.

[11] ILO, "Employment, Incomes and Equality: A strategy for increasing productive employment in Kenya", Geneva, 1973.

[12] Thus, A.S. Oberai, "An analysis of migration into Greater Khartoum", ILO WEP Working Paper, June 1975; and Abdel Rahman Ali

Taha, "Magnitude, characteristics and policy implications of informal sector activities", ILO WEP Working Paper 1975.

[13] For example Birks and Sinclair, "Human capital on the Nile: development and emigration in the Arab Republic of Egypt and the Democratic Republic of the Sudan", WEP Working Paper, Geneva 1978. Their optimistic stance was reiterated in a later book, Arab manpower (London 1981) which is somewhat surprising in view of the many problems which were by then clearly apparent.

[14] See Table A2 in the Appendix for a detailed breakdown of this official figure, by country of destination.

[15] Mohammed El Awad Galal El Din, "Emigration from Sudan abroad" ESRC Khartoum 1979 (in Arabic).

[16] Labour Department records show that the issue of permits to work abroad more than quintupled between 1975/76 and 1980/81.

[17] World Bank, Report on Manpower and International Labour Migration in the Middle East and North Africa, June 1981.

[18] As pointed out by Birks and Sinclair (1981).

[19] Table A3 in the Appendix provided official figures of contracted workers in Saudi Arabia and Libya over 1974-81, broken down by occupation. It shows that less than half of such workers could be considered as unskilled.

[20] This may be related to the fact that it is easier for those with some work experience to get jobs in the destination countries.

[21] See Table A2 in the Appendix.

[22] For example IBRD (1982) op. cit.

[23] This information (in Table A13) must be treated very cautiously as it is prone to error and the level of response in the sample was not always up to the desired standard. But it can be used to give broad indications.

[24] Table A13 also shows substantial variation in pay for the same occupation within Saudi Arabia (especially teachers and administrators). To some extent this is related to the differential rates of pay within Sudan, but this is not always the case. This indicates that the labour market in Saudi Arabia may be fairly segmented or lack channels of information and mobility which would act as wage equalisers within occupational groups.

[25] These issues are taken up in section V.

[26] For example, the Vocational Training Institute in Port Sudan can only enrol less than one-fourth of the total number of applicants.

27 For example, the Union Carbide Company and Rouby Battery Company, in Khartoum, Port Sudan Refinery, and all the texitle mills reported problems in hiring skilled labour. In some cases there were posts left unfilled (for engineers and accountants) because of inability to hire labour.

28 For example, in Port Sudan Refinery, the operations side of the factory faces great difficulty because every year at least 7 (out of a total of 50) skilled machines operators leave, usually to emigrate. Training of new operators may take as long as a year, so that in the meantime production is affected.

29 For example, Asindeco in Khartoum and Abdu Rabo Flour Mill in Port Sudan.

30 An example of the former is Shell Oil Co., of the latter, Mustafa El Amin Oil Mills in Port Sudan.

31 This is a growing practice, e.g. Saeed Food Factory in Khartoum.

32 Thus, Ali Ahmed, Suliman, op. cit.; ILO (1976), op. cit.

33 The 1973 Census estimated the rates of open unemployment in urban Sudan at 5-7 per cent and in Khartoum alone at 5.0 per cent. Apparently, unemployment has been heavily concentrated among the young: the ILO 1976 Report estimated that around 60 per cent of the unemployed were under 25 years, many of them looking for their first job.

34 The survey of establishments, on which this data is based, covered an incomplete sample: methods of collection were not always adequately specified; and there is a suspicion that the exact definition attached to "weekly earnings" etc. (whether inclusive of benefits or not) may have varied between surveys, so that the data is not strictly comparable. Unfortunately, it is the only existing time-series information on wages in the urban sector in the Sudan.

35 For example, M. Murtada Mustafa, Development Planning and International Migration in the Sudan, Labour and Society, January 1980.

36 Statistics from the Labour Department, Khartoum.

37This is understandable, even predictable, given that mahy subisdiary occupations eat into the times specified for main occupation - e.g. government employees who also do private work, often during office hours.

38 In the Saeed Food Factory in Khartoum North, for example, 80 per cent of the unskilled workforce of 500 leaves within 3 months.

39 In the Sudan Textile Compnay, the largest textile factory, 1,000 workers leave every month, while in Port Sudan, the situation is no better. The International Spinning Company has a requirement of

767 workers but in 1982 could only employ 408.   Between 1981 and September 1982 the Company hired 3,071 workers, and 2,420 left.

[40] See Ali Ahmed Suliman, 1971.

[41] For example the Mustafa El Amin Oil Mills in Port Sudan.

[42] This would make it a phenomenon typical of industrial "sickness" - the problems that companies encounter in periods of demand recession, especially if they face other supply constraints as well.   In that case this situation reflects a slow response of industrial investment (in not pulling out of declining sectors fast enough) rather than non-rational behaviour of employers.

[43] Driving taxis appears to be a popular - and remunerative - secondary activity for those with the skill and the means.

[44] The results of the Khartoum Household Expenditure Survey of 1978-80, which was based on a random sample, provide some account of the income and expenditure distribution of the urban population of Khartoum.   These by and large confirm the results of the Labour Market Survey, 1982.

[45] The data in Table 4.3 were not chosen to confirm a pre-existing bias - they include the main occupations held by females covered in the survey.

[46] Unlike in other developing countries, e.g. in South Asia.

[47] A feature that stands out is the relatively advantageous position of refugees.   The reaons for this are discussed in the next section.

[48] For example Khalid Affan, Wage Determination and Structure in Sudan, Sudan Journal of Development Research, February 1977.

[49] For example Ali Abdel Gadir Ali.

[50] This conclusion is confirmed by the Khartoum Household Expenditure Survey of 1978-80 which showed that "own account" average incomes are higher than those of employees.

[51] All from Eritrea/Ethiopia.

[52] The figures are as follows:

	Annual				Hourly	
	Mean	Mode	Max	Min	Mean	Mode
Refugee	2633	2520	5280	1560	0.80	1.01
Sudanese	3290	4200	4200	1920	1.30	

53 This is based on oral evidence rather than any statistical information.

54 Thus for bricklayers the mean for refugees is £S1,616 per year, while for Sudanese it is £S1,310. Those occupations where the refugee wae mean is lower than that for the Sudanese are the following:

Wages per annum	Mean refugee	Mean Sudanese
Salesman	600	786
Carpenter	1200	1707
Clerk	1080	1517

55 Indeed, the Labour Office itself could probably play this role.

56 For example, Port Sudan Refinery, International Tyre Manufacturing and Distribution Company, International Spinning Company, Shell Oil Company. This is also the case in similar capital-intensive factories in Greater Khartoum.

57 See the Skill Survey of Refugees, ILO (1983).

58 The State Electricity Board in Khartoum alone employes over 14,000 people.

59 Thus, for example, the recent discarding of the policy of recruitment of all agriculture graduates has created a situation of unemployment among this group, especially as the universities continue to produce such graduates.

60 For example, that of Port Sudan.

61 There has recently been an increase in the minimum wage in the public sector (now £S40 + 15 per month, from January 1983) but this implies an increase still lower than the rate of inflation.

Appendix to Chapter 4:   Tables

Table A 1:   Present* pay structure, Government and public sector
(monthly wage in £S)

Grade	Government		Public sector	
	Minimum	Maximum	Minimum	Maximum
1	408.33	450	445.80	487.50
2	368.33	398.33	402.50	435.80
3	335	361.66	383.30	413
4	301.66	328.33	365	395
5	268.33	295	346.25	376.25
6	228.33	261.66	327.50	357.50
7	181.66	221.66	285	315
8	125	175	245	282.50
9	83	125	231.60	276.60
10	129.60	164.60	200.80	240.80
11	95.50	124.60	183.30	223.30
12	80.50	108	172.90	212.90
13	65.50	87.50	104.16	150
14	49.60	70.50		
15	47.90	63		
16	41.30	53		
17	35	42		
18	28	37	29.16	40.50

* Note: This has recently been revised, as from January 1983.
The minimum wage has increased from £S28 per month
(+£S12 for transport) to £S40 per month (+£S15 for transport).

Table A 2: Official estimates of Sudanese working abroad

Country	Number in 1977[1]	Number in 1981[2]	% Increase
Egypt	45,000	45,000 [3]	--
Saudi Arabia	140,550	191,830 [4]	36.5
Libya	20,000	32,950 [4]	64.8
Emirates	12,000	26,400	120
Oman	1,800	3,960	120
Qatar	2,500	6,000 [5]	140
North Yemen	800	6,000 [5]	650
Jordan	300	600	200
Bahrain	100	220	120
Lebanon	500	1,000	100
Nigeria	500	1,000	100
United Kingdom	1,500	3,000	100
Greece	300	600	100
Others	2,000	4,000	100
TOTAL	231,350	330,260	42.8

[1] Source: Estimate by Dr. Mohammed El Awad Gelal El Din, Emigration from Sudan Abroad, ESRC Khartoum, 1979.

[2] Source: Estimate by Labour Department, Khartoum, 1982.

[3] According to the Labour Department, Eygpt is now considered an unattractive area for employment.

[4] These estimates are based on the assumption that emigration by contract through the Labour Department account for 70 per cent of the total while the rest is either personal contacts or illegal. Thus these are probably under-estimates.

[5] Actual statistics, rather than estimates.

Table A 3: Contracted Sudanese Workers in Libya and Saudi Arabia

Occupation	1974-78		1978-79		1979-80		1980-81		Total
	SA	Libya	SA	Libya	SA	Libya	SA	Libya	
Technicians	465	134	732	43	950	161	1,154	119	3,763
Managers and Administrators	141	60	220	8	137	16	480	7	1,069
Clerks	284	35	37	3	442	34	177	71	1,083
Service workers	273	135	374	65	170	115	369	72	1,581
Sales workers	--	--	10	2	121	2	129	14	278
Agricultural workers	--	--	38	6	300	6	655	3	1,008
Factory workers	--	29	7	14	70	14	46	5	185
Tailors	17	19	45	8	85	7	54	5	240
Carpenters	379	506	231	41	617	111	412	83	2,380
Blacksmiths	263	241	365	42	363	113	384	53	2,024
Fitters and Mechanics	289	142	28	13	501	97	363	53	1,492
Electricians	195	82	114	20	59	45	397	18	930
Plumbers	121	41	91	14	87	348	87	2	791
Painters	61	90	140	16	551	32	340	36	1,272
Builders	450	485	381	86	412	85	353	128	2,380
Transport workers	1,105	646	747	79	1,616	404	887	165	5,649
Typists	8	11	4	11	163	53	--	--	257
Unskilled workers	2,250	460	2,740	789	5,814	956	4,748	5,190	18,282
Others	229	31	--	--	--	--	--	--	253
TOTAL	6,523	3,155	6,328	1,266	12,658	2,599	4,035	1,353	44,917

Source: Statistics from the Labour Department, Khartoum.

Source for Tables A 4 - A 14: Migration Survey

Table A 4: Age and Sex of Migrants in Survey

		Number	Per Cent
Males:	18-30 years	133	61.6
	31-45 years	61	28.2
	45-60 years	2	0.9
Females:	18-30 years	20	9.3
TOTAL		216	100.0

Table A 5: Region of Origin

	Number	Per cent
Khartoum	45	20.8
Gezira, Blue Nile and White Nile	46	21.3
Kassala	5	2.3
Red Sea	2	0.9
Total Eastern and Central	98	45.4
Northern	52	24.1
Nile Province	10	4.6
Karfur	9	4.2
Kordofan	19	8.8
Total Western	28	13.0
Ethiopia, Eritrea and Tigray	21	9.7
Unspecified	7	3.2
TOTAL	216	100.0

Table A 6: Literacy

	Number	Per cent
Illiterate	25	11.6
Literate in Arabic only	65	30.1
Literate in Arabic and English	102	47.2
Literate in Arabic, English and a third language	9	4.2
Literate in Arabic and one other language (not English)	10	4.6
Literate in other language only	5	2.3

Table A 7: Education

	Number	Per cent	
None	20	9.3	
Khalwa	2	0.9)	
Primary	34	15.7)	32.3
Intermediate	34	15.7)	
Secondary Academic	59	27.3)	
Secondary technical	9	4.2)	
Secondary science	2	0.9)	
BA or MA	26	12.0)	
Science degree	6	2.8)	
Medicine degree	2	0.9)	58.3
Engineering	2	0.9)	
Polytechnic	9	4.2)	
Other diploma	3	1.4)	
Teacher training	6	2.8)	
Ph.D	2	0.9)	
TOTAL	216		

Table A 8: Skills

	Number	Per cent
No skills	81	37.5
Teaching	23	10.6
Accounting	13	6.0
Clerical and typing	25	11.5
Driving	19	8.8
Technical and mechanical	13	6.0
Administration and management	9	4.2
Carpentry and construction	7	3.2
Electrician	4	1.9
Tailor	5	2.3
Other miscellaneous skills	24	11.1

N.B. The numbers add up to more than 216 because some migrants
      have multiple skills.

Table A 9: Occupation in Sudan

	Number	Per cent
Unemployed, searching for job	16	7.4
Student, or not searching for job	14	6.5
Unskilled labourer	31	14.4
Mechanics, Electricians)		
Carpenters, Welders)	20	9.3
Technicians, Blacksmiths)		
White collar employees	36	16.7
Officials and managers	18	8.3
Engineers, Accountants, Doctors		
Doctors and Medical Workers	18	8.3
Others	39	18.1

Table A 10:   Destination of Sample migrants

	Number	Per cent
Saudi Arabia	167	77.3
Kuwait	17	7.9
Qatar	21	9.7
Abu Dhabi	3	1.4
Dubai	1	0.5
Oman	2	0.9
North Yemen	2	0.9
Egypt	1	0.5
West Germany	1	0.5
Any Arab country	1	0.5
TOTAL	216	100.0

Table A 11:   Reasons for choice of desintation of sample migrants

	Number	Per cent
No answer or don't know	123	56.9
Been there before	5	2.3
Family/friends there	29	13.4
Contractor's choice	8	3.7
Best place	4	1.9
Better wages there	23	10.6
Near Sudan	7	3.2
Work facility	12	5.6
Religious incentives	4	1.9
Better living conditions	1	0.5

Table A 12: Offer of Job

	Number	Per cent
No	46	21.3
Yes, total	168	77.8
of which:		
(1) Through contractor	64	38.1
(2) Through family	33	19.6
(3) Through friends	30	17.9
(4) Through own application	21	12.5
(5) Through Government	17	10.1
(6) Through Labour Office	2	1.2
(7) Not specific	1	0.6
No response	2	0.9

For all No, Job Desired

Same as present job	24	52.2
Different job	14	30.4
Don't know or no response	8	17.4

For all Yes, Type of Job

Same as present job	104	61.9
Related skill	5	3.0
Unskilled to other job	28	16.7
Different skill	31	18.4

Table A 13: Present and prospective wages of selected migrants to Saudi Arabia (£S per year)

Present Occupation in Sudan	Present wage in Sudan	Prospective Wage in Saudi Arabia	Present Occupation in Sudan	Present wage in Sudan	Prospective Wage in Saudi Arabia
Teacher	3,060	7,200	University Lecturer/ Professor	2,100	4,800
"	700	4,200	"	10,000	19,200
"	1,200	5,040	"	6,000	21,600
"	1,020	7,200	Doctor	2,112	30,240
"	800	9,000	Blacksmith	1,200	10,800
"	1,800	8,640	"	1,200	7,200
"	840	3,672	Mechanic	2,000	7,200
Labourer	730	2,880	"	3,000	28,800
"	2,160	10,800	"	3,000	8,640
Accountant	900	10,800	Electrician	840	9,600
"	1,500	15,000	"	600	4,500
"	1,440	10,080	"	2,136	7,200
Administrator	1,020	14,400	Driver	1,500	5,600
"	2,000	18,000	"	768	1,200
"	1,500	3,672	"	700	4,320
"	1,500	7,416	"	600	3,600
"	2,160	3,672	"	1,200	5,760
"	720	2,400	"	480	1,440
Secretary	1,025	5,760	Manager	4,180	30,912
Interpreter	840	1,440	Market labourer	762	3,600
Banker	980	11,520	Technician	1,500	4,200
"	1,960	12,960	"	3,000	9,000
Clerk	1,800	14,400	Welder	1,006	7,200
"	684	10,800	Construction worker	500	3,600
			Receptionist	700	1,050
			"	1,500	3,600
			Telephonist	648	9,000
			"		2,880

Table A 14: Emigrants' plan for spending income earned abroad

	Number	Per cent
Marry	24	11.1
Buy urban land/house	75	34.7
Buy a car	27	12.5
Remit	100	46.3
Save (for unspecified use)	41	19.0
Save for eductation	10	4.6
Increase consumption	7	3.2
World travel	1	0.5
Don't know or no response	10	4.6
Productive investment	17	7.9
of which:		
Invest in agricultural land	5	2.3
Start workshop/enterprise	5	2.3
Open shop	4	1.9
Other Trade (e.g. taxi)	3	1.4

(Multiple responses included)

Source: Migration survey.

Table A 15: Graduates of various universities, etc. 1977/78 and 1978/79 (total for 2 years)

Subject	Univ. of Khartoum	Islamic Univ. of Omdurman	Univ. of Juba	Univ. of Gezira	Cairo Univ. Khartoum Branch	Khartoum Polytechnic	Other Colleges and Institutes	Total
Arts	391	354	(students)	(students)	1,070	63	140	2,018
Social sciences, Education and Law	711	129	408	50	1,516	204	22	3,040
Agriculture	403	--	--	66	--	234	307 (students)	1,010
Science	217	--	--	39	12	--	--	268
Engingeering) Medicine) Pharmacology) Veterinary) Architecture, etc.)	1,057	--	19	47	--	451	228	1,802
TOTAL	2,779	483	427	202	2,598	952	697	8,138

Source: Statistical Abstract of Sudan, 1981, p. 37-49.

Table A 16:   Shortages of professional and skilled manpower
              officially estimated for 1977-78 to 1982-83 by Government

Professionals:

Agriculturalists	2,340
Veterinary Doctors	1,200
Engineers	2,160
Total	5,700

Technicians:

Agriculture and forestry	2,850
Veterinary	1,420
Medical Assistants	1,030
Mechanical and Electrical	2,920
Technical and Construction	1,650
Total	9,870

Assistant Technicians:

Agriculture, Forestry and Veterinary	2,200
Mechanics and Chemists	1,100
Construction	2,100
Total	5,730
Grand Total	21,300

Source: Sudan Country Presentation to the UNDP Conference
          on LDCs, Paris, UN 1981.

Table A 17: Characteristics of household by wage
             of household head

Wage brackets for household head	Average size of household	Average Dependent - Earner ratio	Number of households
200	8.0	2.44	4
201-400	6.38	1.60	29
401-500	6.13	2.99	15
501-600	5.36	2.27	36
601-800	5.26	2.67	96
801-1000	5.90	3.19	113
1001-1500	5.08	3.03	182
1501-2400	5.68	2.95	148
2401-6000	5.70	3.39	120
6000	5.86	2.89	14

Average wage of
Household

200	--	--	--
201-400	5.27	2.2	11
401-500	6.72	2.92	25
501-600	5.58	2.79	38
601-800	5.40	2.57	106
801-1000	6.13	3.17	129
1001-1500	5.36	2.90	211
1501-2400	5.57	2.90	148
2401-6000	5.60	3.37	121
6000	6.44	2.51	18

Source: Urban Labour Market Survey

Table A 18: Wage brackets for main occupation: (% Distribution)

Wages (£S)	Managers	Professionals	Teachers	Government	Secretarial clerical admin.	Skilled workers	Own trade	Production workers	Service workers	Farmers	Other	Total
< 200	--	--	--	--	--	--	--	--	--	11.11	--	0.9
200-400	--	1.79	--	--	0.92	1.93	3.08	5.63	7.83	32.41	--	6.10
401-500	--	--	--	--	0.92	1.69	--	5.96	5.07	8.33	--	3.46
501-600	--	--	--	--	1.83	4.34	--	12.25	11.52	4.63	--	6.55
601-800	--	1.79	35.29	21.05	10.09	10.36	7.69	17.88	21.20	16.67	--	14.16
801-1000	--	5.36	29.41	15.79	19.27	12.77	7.69	17.55	17.51	12.04	--	14.61
1001-1500	--	12.50	17.65	21.05	22.94	28.43	21.54	26.16	15.21	4.63	100	21.76
1501-2400	5.26	28.57	5.88	31.58	22.02	23.86	24.62	9.27	11.52	5.56	--	16.72
2401-6000	68.42	42.86	5.88	10.53	19.27	14.22	26.15	5.3	6.45	3.70	--	12.88
> 6000	26.32	7.14	5.88	--	2.75	2.41	9.23	--	3.69	0.93	--	2.86
Total Number	19	56	17	19	109	415	65	302	217	108	1	1,328
% of sample	1.43	4.22	1.28	1.43	8.21	31.25	4.89	22.74	16.34	8.13	0.08	100

Source: Urban Labour Market Survey.

Table A 19: Wages by sex - main occupational groups (% distribution)

Wage Brackets (£S)	Professional and White Collar		Skilled workers		Unskilled workers	
	Male	Female	Male	Female	Male	Female
200-400	0.54	2.78	1.72	14.29	6.13	10.71
401-500	0.54	--	1.47	14.29	5.15	19.23
501-600	1.09	--	3.68	42.86	10.78	21.43
601-800	7.07	25.0	10.29	14.29	17.89	17.98
801-1000	13.59	19.44	12.99	--	17.16	2.78
1001-1500	17.93	16.67	28.92	--	23.53	3.03
1501-2400	22.83	16.67	24.26	--	11.27	6.12
2401-6000	29.35	19.44	14.22	14.29	6.86	3.45
> 6000	7.07	--	2.45	--	1.23	--
Total No.	184	36	408	7	408	45
% of sample	83.64	16.36	98.31	1.69	90.07	9.93

Source: Urban Labour Market Survey.

Table A 20: __Wages by region:__ (% Distribution)

Regions	Professional and white collar				Unskilled workers				Skilled workers			
	< 500 %	501-1000 %	>1000 %	Total number	< 500 %	501-1000 %	> 1000 %	Total number	< 500 %	501-1000 %	>1000 %	Total number
Central	2.6	22.8	74.6	114	14.8	47.4	37.8	135	6.1	23.3	70.6	163
Eastern	--	45.0	55.0	40	12.0	49.0	39.0	100	1.5	24.6	73.9	65
Northern	--	16.1	83.9	31	6.2	37.5	56.3	48	--	26.9	73.1	52
Southern	--	30.8	69.2	13	11.3	53.2	35.5	62	5	27.5	67.5	40
Western	--	15.0	85.0	20	10.9	51.5	37.6	101	2.4	42.2	55.4	83
Refugee	--	--	100.0	2	20.0	--	80.0	5	--	--	100	11
Other	--	--	--	--	--	50.0	50.0	2	--	--	100	1
Total	1.3	25.5	73.2	220	11.9	47.9	40.2	453	3.6	27.5	68.9	415

__Source:__ Urban Labour Market Survey

Table A 21: Wages by education: (% distribution)

Education level	Professional and white collar				Skilled workers				Unskilled workers			
	<500 %	501-1000 %	>1000 %	Total number	<500 %	501-1000 %	>1000 %	Total number	<500 %	501-1000 %	>1000 %	Total number
No education	--	33.3	66.6	3 (1.4)	5.6	37.1	57.3	89 (21.5)	13.5	51.5	35.0	171 (37.8)
Primary School	10.0	30.0	60.0	10 (4.6)	3.0	28.4	68.6	169 (40.7)	9.9	43.2	46.9	162 (35.8)
Intermediate	3.3	26.7	60.0	30 (13.6)	5.6	29.9	64.5	87 (21.0)	15.4	53.8	30.8	78 (17.2)
Secondary School	1.0	39.8	59.2	98 (44.6)	--	11.5	88.5	61 (14.7)	9.4	50.0	40.6	32 (7.1)
Arts degree	--	8.1	91.9	37 (16.8)	--	--	100	1 (0.2)	--	--	100	2 (0.4)
Polytechnic or other	--	11.1	88.9	18 (8.2)	--	--	100	5 (1.2)	--	100	--	1 (0.2)
Science, medicine, engineering	--	--	100	24 (10.9)	--	--	100	3 (0.7)	--	--	100	7 (1.6)
TOTAL	1.4	25.5	73.1	220	3.6	27.5	68.9	415	11.9	47.9	40.2	453

Source: Urban Labour Market Survey.

Table A 22 (A): Wage by type of employer: Skilled workers (% Distribution)

Wage Bracket	Self Employed	Government	Public Sector	Large Private Company	Small Private Company	Private Individual	Other	Total Number
200-400	2.5	--	4.8	0.6	4.1	1.7	--	1.9
401-500	1.2	4.2	--	0.6	6.1	1.7	--	1.7
501-600	2.5	8.3	--	5.6	--	8.5	--	4.3
601-800	6.2	8.3	14.3	10.0	14.3	11.9	--	10.4
801-1000	5.0	37.5	21.4	12.5	10.2	10.2	--	12.8
1001-1500	17.5	25.0	26.2	35.0	30.6	27.1	--	28.4
1501-2400	38.8	16.7	19.1	19.4	18.4	27.1	--	23.9
2401-6000	23.8	--	9.5	13.8	16.3	8.5	100	14.2
> 6000	2.5	--	4.8	2.5	--	3.4	--	2.4
Total	80 (19.3)	24 (5.8)	42 (10.1)	160 (38.6)	49 (11.8)	59 (14.2)	1 (0.2)	415

Table A 22 (B): Wage by type of employer: Unskilled workers (% Distribution)

Wage Bracket	Self Employed	Government	Public Sector	Large Private Company	Small Private Company	Private Individual	Other	Total Number
200-400	5.6	13.0	14.3	3.1	8.3	9.3	--	6.2
401-500	4.2	2.2	9.5	6.2	10.4	3.7	5.3	5.8
501-600	4.2	15.2	--	13.5	27.1	13.0	--	12.4
601-800	7.0	15.2	23.8	25.9	29.2	5.6	15.8	19.7
801-1000	9.9	13.0	28.6	15.0	14.6	33.3	15.8	15.7
1001-1500	25.4	15.2	19.1	23.3	4.2	13.0	57.9	21.9
1501-2400	22.5	15.2	4.8	7.3	4.2	16.7	--	10.8
2401-6000	18.3	6.5	--	5.7	2.1	1.9	--	6.4
> 6000	2.8	4.4	--	--	--	--	5.3	1.1
Total	71 (15.7)	46 (10.2)	21 (4.7)	193 (42.7)	48 (10.6)	54 (11.9)	19 (4.2)	452

Table A 22 (C): Wage by type of employer: Professional and white collar (% Distribution)

Wage Bracket	Self Employed	Government	Public Sector	Large Private Company	Small Private Company	Private Individual	Other	Total Number
200-400	--	1.7	--	--	7.7	--	--	0.9
401-500	--	--	4.2	--	--	--	--	0.5
501-600	--	--	4.2	0.9	--	--	--	0.9
601-800	--	25.4	8.33	2.6	9.1	--	--	10.0
801-100	--	27.1	12.5	7.0	6.3	100	50	14.6
1001-1500	33.3	22.0	25.0	16.5	--	--	--	17.7
1501-2400	--	16.9	25.0	25.2	4.2	--	--	21.8
2401-6000	66.7	6.8	20.8	40.9	4.9	--	--	27.7
> 6000	--	--	--	7.0	23.1	--	50	5.9
Total	3 (1.4)	59 (26.8)	24 (10.9)	115 (52.3)	13 (5.9)	2 (0.9)	2 (0.9)	220

Table A 23: Workers by type of contract (% Distribution)

	Daily	Fortnightly Weekly Monthly	Seasonal	Annual	Salaried	Task Work	Piece Work	Total
Professionals	--	--	1.9	24.1	72.2	--	--	54
Government	--	5.6	5.6	16.7	72.2	--	--	18
Managers	--	--	--	6.2	93.8	--	--	16
Teachers	--	--	--	23.5	76.5	--	--	17
Secretarial Clerical Administrative	--	0.9	1.9	4.6	88.0	0.9	3.7	108
Skilled Workers	5.3	2.5	1.0	12.7	65.2	1.8	11.4	394
Production Workers	11.0	6.7	1.7	8.7	60.9	1.0	10.0	299
Service workers	4.2	1.4	2.4	16.4	58.7	3.8	13.2	213
Total	5.7	2.9	6.1	13.1	60.4	1.9	9.9	1,251

Table A 24: Average Weekly Earnings in Private Sector

Type of Activity	1973 Establishments with > 5 employees			1975 Establishments with >10 employees			1979 Establishment with > 10 employees		
	Wage earner	Salaried	All	Wage earner	Salaried	All	Wage earner	Salaried	All
Manufacture of food, beverage, tobacco	3.99	14.09	4.85	4.47	16.82	5.67	18.84	30.49	20.03
Textile, apparel and leather	4.35	11.89	5.00	5.64	9.74	6.01	13.56	21.38	14.49
Wood and wood products	4.62	17.82	5.26	13.77	11.94	13.50	12.37	22.05	13.76
Paper and paper products	4.90	11.53	5.91	5.31	17.43	6.83	12.10	20.26	13.36
Chemicals and chemical products and petroleum	6.48	20.56	7.16	5.6	16.34	6.73	11.81	35.35	14.67
Non-material mineral products except petroleum and coal	4.71	21.30	6.27	4.14	18.06	5.35	11.47	31.11	12.88
Fabricated metal, machinery and equipment	4.42	17.51	5.28	5.62	19.14	6.59	14.80	30.69	17.40
Other manufacturing	3.07	13.80	3.83	2.92	11.44	3.97	12.09	34.20	13.43
Total manufacturing	4.36	14.63	5.29	5.40	14.17	6.28	14.92	26.78	16.24
Electricity, gas and water	7.20	7.13	7.18				18.66	41.06	33.78
Construction	4.60	13.29	5.11	5.51	16.32	6.44	12.27	31.54	13.64
Wholesale trade	5.40	18.21	9.28	7.76	19.84	11.77	13.93	33.04	19.26
Retail trade	5.39	17.55	9.69	5.41	14.28	28.29	18.25	26.48	22.70
Restaurants and hotels	4.46	8.24	4.63	2.71	6.80	3.01	10.89	22.90	12.35
Total trade	5.04	17.36	7.92	5.19	17.12	8.07	12.79	30.94	16.95
Transport and storage and communications	5.88	17.38	9.97	1.13	6.14	1.71	14.13	37.25	30.64
Finance	5.92	19.93	15.43	5.38	4.68	5.13	16.40	50.33	39.42
Insurance	4.10	16.91	13.44	6.48	8.42	8.08	12.04	27.01	23.80
Real estate and business	3.54	16.24	7.77	3.54	14.17	5.21	12.19	33.89	25.63

Source: Department of labour, Khartoum Manpower Surveys

Table A 25: (a) Wage brackets by size of firm: skilled workers % of Total (Rows)

Size of firm	200-400	401-500	501-600	601-800	801-1000	1001-1500	1501-2400	2401-6000	>6000	Total Number
Very small <50	--	--	--	40.0	--	20.0	20.0	20.0	--	5
Small 51-100	11.11	5.56	11.11	22.22	2.78	22.22	11.11	11.11	2.78	36
Medium 101-300	--	--	--	--	14.81	33.33	22.22	25.93	3.7	27
Big 301-1000	1.89	--	3.77	9.43	7.55	32.08	32.08	7.55	5.66	53
Large 1001-5000	--	--	--	--	20.0	20.0	20.0	40.0	--	5
Very large >5000	2.41	1.2	4.82	9.64	18.07	36.14	22.89	4.82	--	83
Other	0.62	2.48	3.73	9.94	12.42	22.98	23.6	21.12	3.11	1.61
Total number	2.16	1.89	4.32	10.54	12.16	27.84	23.24	15.14	2.7	3.70

(b) Wage brackets by size of firm: Production workers % of total (Rows)

Size of firm	200-400	401-500	501-600	601-800	801-1000	1001-1500	1501-2400	2401-6000	>6000	Total Number
Very small <50	50.0	--	16.67	16.67	--	16.67	--	--	--	6
Small 51-100	3.13	6.26	25.0	28.13	9.38	18.75	9.38	--	--	32
Medium 101-300	--	--	3.7	11.11	18.52	22.22	22.22	22.22	--	27
Big 301-1000	5.56	6.94	23.61	15.28	11.11	26.39	9.72	1.39	--	72
Large 1001-5000	--	--	--	15.38	23.08	53.85	7.69	--	--	26
Very large >5000	6.12	6.12	8.16	22.45	28.57	22.45	4.08	2.04	--	49
Other	5.41	7.21	5.41	14.41	20.72	28.83	9.91	8.11	--	111
Total	5.26	5.57	11.46	17.03	18.27	27.55	9.6	5.26	--	323

Table A 26:   Sample Households: Income Data

Income Brackets	Income per Capita		Income per adult equiv.[1]	
	Number	Per cent	Number	Per cent
< 200	180	22.31	134	16.60
200-400	245	30.36	256	31.72
401-500	71	8.80	85	10.53
501-600	59	7.31	62	7.68
601-800	63	7.81	87	10.78
801-1000	54	6.69	41	5.08
1001-1500	71	8.80	85	10.53
1501-2400	36	4.46	30	3.72
2401-6000	25	3.10	23	2.85
> 6000	3	0.37	4	0.50

[1] The following adult equivalent weights were used:

Age Group	Males	Females
< 5		0.45
5-9		0.6
10-14		0.85
15-29	1.2	1.0
30-59	1.0	0.88
60 +	0.88	0.72

Table A 27: Commodity prices, free market, Khartoum
July 1982
(£S)

Mutton, kg.	4.750
Other meat, kg.	3.750
Fish, kg.	2.000
1 dozen eggs	2.125
Cheese	4.750
Tomatoes, kg.,	2.250
Potatoes, kg.	0.750
Bamia, kg.	0.600
Kosa, kg.	8.000
Onion, kg	1.250
Molokhia, kg.	0.400
Lemon, kg.	0.500
Sorghum (robo)	2.500
1 loaf bread	0.120
Coffee (1 lb.)	2.750
Washing soap, 1 bar	0.115
Oil tin (5 litres)	7.000
Coal (sack)	6.000

Note: Unfortunately, the official prices of these commodities were
not available. However the official prices are on the whole
much lower than those prevailing in the free market. This
means that the cost of living indices, which are based on
official prices, have a strong bias towards underestimation.

ANNEXES

Glossary

Ardeb	A crop measure: 1 ardeb = 2-ninety kilo bags
Bildat	Small to medium-sized holdings of rainfed cropped land
Buda	Striga Hermonthica, a form of parasitic weed
Dura	Sorghum
Feddan	A measure of land: 1 feddan = 1.04 acres or 0.42 hectares
Gereif	River flood land
Nafir	Communal free labour
Piastre	100 piastres = 1 Sudanese pound
Sheil	A form of crop mortgage which is the major form of private moneylending in rural areas
Shiakha	A socio-political grouping within villages, based on tribal affiliation and headed by a sheikh
£S	Sudanese pound: £S1.3 = US$1.00 in September 1982
Souk	Market
Tulba	Labour hired by a block inspector on an irrigated scheme, and allocated to the account of a tenant.

N.B. "The Sudan" is referred to in this volume as Sudan, and "Libyan Arab Jamahiriya" as Libya. One billion stands for thousands of millions.

Select Bibliography

Abdel Hamid, Ahmed (1966). Agricultural Labour in the Gezira Scheme, Sudan Gezira Board Social Research Section.

Abdel Rahim, A.W. (1968). An Economic History of the Gezira Scheme: 1900-1956, unpublished Ph.D. thesis, University of Manchester.

Adam, F.H. (1970). The Sharing Arrangement in Three Agricultural Corporations of the Public Sector in Sudanese Agriculture, University of Khartoum, Department of Rural Economy.

Adams, Martin E. ; Howell, John (1979). Developing the Traditional Sector in the Sudan, Economic Development and Cultural Change, Vol. 27, No.3, April.

Affan, Khalid (1977). Wage Determination and Structure in Sudan, Sudan Journal of Development Research, February.

---. (1978). Output, Employment and Income Distribution in Mechanised Farming: A report on the findings of a socio-economic survey in Habila, Southern Kordofan, ILO Geneva.

Ahmed, S.A. (1977). The Integration of Agricultural Credit and Marketing in the Gezira Scheme of the Sudan, unpublished PH.D. thesis, University of London.

Ali, A. Abdel Gadir (1983). The Labour Market in the Gezira Scheme, mimeo, ILO Geneva.

Ali Taha, Abdel Rahman (1975). Magnitude, characteristics and policy implications of informal sector activities, ILO/WEP Working Paper, Geneva.

Asad, T. (1970). The Kabbabish Arabs, London.

Barbour, K.M. (1980). The Sudan since Independence, Journal of Modern African Studies, Vol. 18, No. 1, March.

Barnett, Tony (1977). The Gezira Scheme: An illusion of development, London.

Barth, F. (1968). Nomads of South Persia, Massachusetts.

Birks, J.A.; Sinclair, T. (1978). Human Capital on the Nile: Development and emigration in the Arab Republic of Egypt and the Democratic Republic of Sudan, ILO/WEP Working Paper, Geneva.

---. (1981). Arab Manpower, London.

Brausch, G.; Crooke, J.; Shaw, D.J. (1963).   Bashagra Arab
    Settlements, University of Khartoum.

Cunnison, I.G. (1966).   Baggara Arabs, Oxford.

Culwick, G.M.   A study of the Human Factor in the Gezira Scheme,
    unpublished report.

Democratic Republic of Sudan (1968).   Agricultural Census 1964-65,
    Department of Statistics, Khartoum.

---. (1973).   Census, Department of Statistics, Khartoum.

---. (1977).   The Six-Year Plan of Ecnomic and Social Development,
    1977/78 to 1982/83, Ministry of National Planning, Khartoum,
    2 volumes.

---.   Statistical Abstracts, 1981 and 1982, Department of Statistics,
    Khartoum.

Duffield, M. (1981).   Maiurno: Capitalism and Rural Life in Sudan,
    London.

Elamin, Abdalla and Ahmed Elbedawi (1981).   Annual Report of Field
    Crop Economic Surveys: Season 1980/81, Sudan Gezira Board
    Economic and Social Research Unit, Barakat.

El Hassan, Ali Mohammed, editor (1975).   Growth, Employment and
    Equity, Khartoum.

Euroconsult (1982).   In association with Alexander Gibbs and Partners
    and TCS Sudan, Ltd. - Gezira Rehabilitation and Modernisation
    Project.

Gaitskell, Arthur (1959).   Gezira: A Story of Development in the
    Sudan, London.

Galal El Din, Mohammed El Awad (1979).   Emigration from Sudan Abroad,
    Economic and Social Research Council, Khartoum (in Arabic).

Holt, P.M. and Daly, J. (19).   The History of the Sudan, London.

IBRD (1979).   Sudan Agricultural Sector Survey, 3 volumes, Washington
    (D.C.).

--- (1982).   Sudan: Planning for Stabilization and Change, Washington
    (D.C.).

ILO/UNDP (1976).   Growth, Employment and Equity: A comprehensive
    strategy for the Sudan, Geneva.

Keddeman, W.; Ali Abdel Gadir Ali (1978).   Employment, Productivity
    and Income in Rural Sudan, Khartoum.

Murtada Mustafa, M. (1980). Development Planning and International Migration in the Sudan, Labour and Society, January.

Nigam, S.B.L. (1977). The Labour Requirement and Supply Situation in Agriculture in the Sudan, in A.M. El Hassan, ed.

O'Brien, Jay (1983a). The Political Economy ofr Capitalist Agriculture in the Central Rainlands of Sudan, Labour Capital and Society, Vol. 16 No. 1, April.

---. (1983b). Formation of the Agricultural Labour Force, Review of African Political Economy No. 26: Special Issue on Sudan, July.

Oberai, A.S. (1975). An Analysis of Migration into Greater Khartoum, ILO/WEP Working Paper, June.

Shugeiry, S.A. (1981). Sharecropping Arrangements and Pricing Policies in the Irrigation of Agriculture: The case of the Gezira Scheme, unpublished M.A. thesis, Institute of Social Sciences, The Hague.

Simpson, I.G.; Simpson, Morag C. (1978). Alternative Strategies for Agricultural Development in the Central Rainlands of the Sudan, Leeds.

Sudan Gezira Board. Statistical Bulletins.

Suleiman, Ali Ahmed (1975). Issues in the Economic Development of the Sudan, Khartoum.

Tothill, J.D. (1948). Agriculture in the Sudan, London.

Toulmin, C. (1983). Equality in Pastoral Societies: Investigating the distribution of livestock in pastoral societies - some problems of definition and method, mimeo, School of Development Studies, University of East Anglia.

Structure of the Project

I. **Coordinating Committee**

- Ambassador Abdel Magid Beshir El-Ahmadi, Commissioner for Refugees
- Mr. Mohammed El-Murtada Mustafa, Commissioner of Labour
- Mr. Samir Radwan, Senior Econommist, ILO
- Mr. Abdul Mejid Hussein, Project Coordinator

II. **Field Officers**

- Mr. Hassan Mohammed Osman, Projects General Manager, Commissioner of Refugees, Eastern Region
- Mr. Ahmed El-Amin, Director of Labour, Eastern Region, Kassala
- Mr. El Tureifi Younis, Projects Deputy General Manager, Commission of Refugees, Showak
- Mr. Ismaeel Ibrahim, Assistant Commissioner for Refugees, Gedaref
- Mr. Abdel Qadir Ibrahim, Assistant Commissioner for Refugees, Port Sudan
- Mr. Mohammed Habib Mirghani, Assistant Commissioner for Refugees, Kassala

Five surveys were carried out in central and eastern Sudan between August and November 1982. Two related to urban labour: one based on a long questionnaire applied to 804 workers in Khartoum, Port Sudan and Kenana; and the second being a small survey of labour emigrants from Sudan carried out in Khartoum. For the rural sector, there were three surveys. Two of them used an identical long questionnaire, applied separately to cultivators in the rainfed farming areas and in the irrigated schemes. The fifth survey was a brief one related to migrant labourers working in the mechanised rainfed agricultural schemes. The following people were involved in the surveys:

Rural rainfed agriculture:

Organisers:

Jennie Dey

and Ibrahim El Bagir

Interviewers:

Mervat Mohammed Abdel Aziz

Kamal Tagelsir El Sheikh

Mohammed Osman Ali

Mirghani Mohamed Daishab

Hashim Mohammed Ali Mosaad

Mohamed Hasan Abdelaziz

Mansour Mahmoud Ahmed

Nadir El Amin

Irrigated Agriculture:

Organisers:

Anthony Barnett

and Taha El Jack Taha

Interviewers:

The same as above, as well as Ibrahim Addoash

Urban:

Organisers:

Jayati Ghosh

and Mohammed Tahir Mageit

Interviewers:

Ayad Matta George

Suhair Ahmed Osman

Suad Mohammed

Abdelgadir

Leila Ibrahim

Abdelmagid Abdelgadir

Hanim Abdallah